EDUCATIONAL REFORM AND ITS CONSEQUENCES

IPPR/Rivers Oram Press

EDUCATIONAL REFORM AND ITS CONSEQUENCES

Edited by
Sally Tomlinson

IPPR/Rivers Oram Press
London

First published in 1994 by
Rivers Oram Press
144 Hemingford Road, London N1 1DE

Published in the USA by
Paul and Company
Post Office Box 442, Concord, MA 01742

Set in 10/12 Sabon by Except*detail* Ltd, Southport
and printed in Great Britain
by T.J. Press (Padstow) Ltd, Padstow, Cornwall

British Library Cataloguing in Publication Data
A catalogue record for this book is available from the British
Library

ISBN 1-85489-064 6
ISBN 1-85489-065 4 pbk

CONTENTS

Contents

ABBREVIATIONS

AEN	Additional Educational Needs
APU	Assessment of Performance Unit
AT	Attainment Targets
BEd	Bachelor of Education
BTEC	Business and Technical Education Council
CATE	Council for the Accreditation of Teacher Education
CILNTEC	Central and Inner London North Training and Enterprise Council
CNAA	Council for National Academic Awards
CPVE	Certificate of Prevocational Education
CTC	City Technology College
DES	Department of Education and Science
DFE	Department for Education
ERA	Education Reform Act 1988
ESRC	Economic and Social Research Council
FEU	Further Education Unit
FSM	Free School Meals
GM	Grant-Maintained
GNVQ	General National Vocational Qualifications
HMI	Her Majesty's Inspectorate
INSET	In-service Teacher Education
IPPR	Institute of Public Policy Research
IT	Information Technology
ITT	Initial Teacher Training
LEA	Local Education Authority
LMS	Local Management of Schools
NCC	National Curriculum Council
NVQ	National Vocational Qualifications
OFSTED	Office of Standards in Education
PGCE	Post-Graduate Certificate of Education
QTS	Qualified Teacher Status

RE	Religious Education
SAT	Standard Assessment Task
SCAA	Schools Curriculum and Assessment Authority
SCI	Senior Chief Inspector
SEAC	Schools Examination and Assessment Council
SEN	Special Educational Needs
TEC	Training and Enterprise Council
TGAT	Test Group on Assessment and Testing
TVEI	Technical and Vocational Education Initiative
UCP	(Hamlyn Post-16) Unified Curriculum Project
ULIE	University of London Institute of Education

LIST OF CONTRIBUTORS

Stephen J. Ball is Professor of Education at the Centre for Educational Studies, King's College, London. He has published widely in the field of the sociology of education, most recently *Politics and Policy-Making in Education: Explorations in Policy Sociology*, Routledge, 1990 and, with Richard Bowe and Anne Gold, *Reforming Education and Changing Schools: Case Studies in Policy Sociology*, Routledge, 1992.

Paul Black is Professor of Science Education at King's College, London. He was chair of the Task Group on Assessment and Testing in 1987/88, and Deputy Chair of the National Curriculum Council from 1988 until 1991.

Eric Bolton is Professor for Teacher Education at the University of London Institute of Education; prior to that he was for nineteen years one of HM Inspectors of Schools, and from 1983 to 1991 the Senior Chief Inspector and head of HMI in England.

Richard Bowe is a Research Officer at the Centre for Educational Studies, King's College, London. He has published work in the areas of school examinations and in the Technical and Vocational Educational Initiative, his most recent publication being *Reforming Education and Changing Schools: Case Studies in Policy Sociology*, Routledge, 1992, with Stephen J. Ball and Anne Gold.

Alison Bullock is a Research Fellow at the School of Education, University of Birmingham. She has worked recently on a project funded by the Leverhulme Trust on 'The Funding of Schools after the 1988 Education Reform Act'. At present she is researching 'The Impact of Local Management on Schools', a major study funded by the National Association of Head Teachers.

John Fitz is Lecturer in Educational Management and Policy, School of Education, University of Wales, Cardiff. He is co-director of an

ESRC-supported project investigating grant-maintained schools policy and the effects of institutional autonomy on school organisation and management.

Sharon Gewirtz is a Research Officer at King's College, London where she is working on an ESRC-funded study of market forces in secondary education. She has published mainly in the field of education policy and is co-author of *Specialisation and Choice in Urban Education: The City Technology College Experiment*, 1993.

David Halpin is a lecturer in education policy and school management at the University of Warwick and author of numerous articles on aspects of the National Curriculum, comprehensive schooling and grant-maintained schools policy.

Annette Hayton is Resource Officer of the Post-16 Education Centre, Institute of Education, University of London.

Ann Hodgson is the Research Officer on the Hamlyn Post-16 Unified Curriculum Project based at the Post-16 Education Centre of London University's Institute of Education. She also works as a Technical and Vocational Educational Initiative Adviser in the London Borough of Tower Hamlets, where she has been particularly involved with the development of a Unified Guidance, Achievement and Progression Framework for Tower Hamlets.

Pat Mahony is Head of the Department of Educational Studies at Goldsmiths' College, London. She is involved in a number of projects funded by local education authorities to research and develop a profile of competences for Newly Qualified Teachers.

Andrew Morris is Assistant Director at City and Islington College (formerly Islington Sixth Form Centre). He was recently seconded to the Institute of Education where he undertook research on a unified post-16 curriculum and initiated the Hamlyn/CILNTEC Post-16 Unified Curriculum Project.

Philip O'Hear, Headteacher of Acland Burghley School in Camden, London, teaches English and has contributed to national developments in GCSE. With John White, he has written on the National Curriculum for the IPPR (1991) and edited *Assessing the National Curriculum*, Paul Chapman, 1993.

Sally Power is a Research Fellow at the University of Warwick working on the Grant-Maintained Schools Research Project. She has published articles on changes in the secondary school curriculum and recent educational policy.

Stewart Ranson is Professor of Education at the University of Birmingham. His work over the past decade has focused on the changing government of education, and the creation of a 'Learning Society'.

Hywel Thomas is Professor of Economics of Education and Head of the School of Education, University of Birmingham. He has researched and written on issues in the finance, regulation and management of delegation in schools.

Sally Tomlinson is Professor of Educational Policy and Management at Goldsmiths' College, London. She has written and researched in the areas of alternative educational policy, effective schooling, special education and the education of ethnic minorities.

Michael Young, one of the co-authors of *A British Baccalaureate: Ending the Division between Education and Training* (IPPR), is Head of the Post-16 Education Centre, Institute of Education, University of London.

Geoff Whitty is Karl Mannheim Professor of the Sociology of Education and Chair of the Department of Policy Studies at the Institute of Education, University of London. He is co-director of the ESRC-funded 'Modes of Teacher Education' project.

PREFACE

The Education Act of 1988 was the culmination, though not the end, of reforms that were genuinely radical. They represented a break from a cumulative, consensual style of development to an alternative set of ideas that were imposed with little consultation and less consent from the mainstream of education. They included the introduction of a quasi-market among schools, the devolution of management, a reduced role for education authorities, and much stronger central control over finance and above all over the content of education. The Act coincided with the foundation of IPPR and from the beginning we were concerned to see how these reforms would work in practice and what might be done to adapt or change them if they did not succeed in raising the quality of education for all pupils. The chapters in this book address both questions, first on the basis of careful observation of what has been happening in schools and second by reflection and suggestion as to how the effects may be either mitigated or improved. The aim of all contributors is to see how we may evolve a system of learning which is open, flexible, comprehensive and capable of offering to all at every stage of their lives from nursery to retirement the opportunity to develop their talents and to acquire the skills necessary to participate successfully in the labour market.

IPPR is greatly indebted to the authors for drawing on their research and experience to throw common light on these questions but especially to Sally Tomlinson. She has been associated with IPPR's educational work from the beginning. She organised the seminar in March 1993 at which these papers were discussed and we are grateful to the Leverhulme Trust for providing funding for the occasion.

James Cornford
Former Director
Institute of Public Policy Research

INTRODUCTION: EDUCATIONAL REFORMS— IDEOLOGIES AND VISIONS

Sally Tomlinson

Over the past decade we have been living through the most comprehensive reworking of the education system since the 1940s. These
changes have not been the result of debate, consensus or reference to
educational research. The pace of legislation; the politicisation of all
aspects of education; the lack of consultation with all but a few select
participants in the education service; the reversals and confusion as
many of the reforms falter; the use of legislation to bolster failing
policies, have left many critics feeling powerless to influence change.
Strategies for opposing reforms, slowing the pace of change, and
presenting alternative policies have been difficult to find, especially as
many potential academic critics have often had their attention
diverted to securing their own, their colleagues', and in some cases,
their institution's survival.

No area of education has escaped the Conservative government's
reforming zeal. The relationship between central and local authority,
school structures, funding and resourcing, curriculum, pedagogy,
assessment, relationships with parents, early years and post-16, modes
of inspection, ancillary services, higher education and teacher training,
have all been subject to scrutiny, criticism and legislation. One view
of all this is that many of the reforms are now entrenched and will be
difficult to reverse, particularly as they are changing not only the
structures and content, but also the principles and values underlying
the education system. Others take the view that the more inequitable
aspects of the reforms will be readily amenable to change as the
resulting educational, social and economic costs become more apparent.

Political opposition to government educational policies is begin-
ning to emerge in the shape of the production of alternative policies.
The Labour Party published a consultation paper on education in
September 1993 (Labour Party 1993) updated in July 1994 and is

engaging in a process of consultation with interested groups and individuals, and left-leaning Professors of Education have published alternative visions of the education service (IPPR 1993, Tomlinson 1993). However, in order to maximise the positive effects of any alternative policies, research and analysis of the effect of current ideologies and reforms are necessary, otherwise there is the possibility that one set of ideologically-based (right-wing) policies could simply be replaced by another (left-wing) set. The production of alternative education policies should ideally be informed by policy-related research. The educational reforms of the 1980s and 1990s have not been notable for their grounding in research findings, and a large parliamentary majority has enabled government to push through policies whose nature and possible outcomes were unresearched. Indeed, Ministers of Education have been at pains to distance themselves from research, even that which they themselves commissioned, when the results did not accord with ideological preference. The problematic implementation of many of the reforms, notably those relating to curriculum and assessment, parental choice, the impact of market competition on schools and pupils, and the effects of the erosion of local democracy, is largely because research on these issues was not commissioned, or research results were used only in support of preconceived policies.

Since 1988 educational researchers have made considerable efforts to carry out funded and unfunded research into the effects of educational reforms. They have attempted to chart the successes and failures of policies, to discover whether the policy effects were in accordance with stated government expectations, or whether unforeseen consequences have emerged (particularly where these are detrimental or advantageous to particular groups of pupils, parents or schools) and have also tried to understand the educational reforms as part of a wider agenda of social and political change.

The papers published here are based on those presented at an invited seminar sponsored by the Leverhulme Trust, held to bring together some of those researching the effects of Conservative policies, and considering alternatives. The seminar, jointly organised by the Institute for Public Policy Research and Goldsmiths' College, University of London, was held at the Ibis Hotel, Euston, on 25–6 March 1993.

Three main conclusions reached during the seminar were that alternative educational policies should:

- be based on clear principles and an explicit value base;
- be based on more extensive research and analysis than is at present available;
- emerge following wide consultation with interested bodies, particularly those who will be implementing policies.

The conference was based on the assumption that alternative policies should be worked out and that we should be able to articulate a version of education for a democratic society that is not built on inappropriate ideology and on policies which are likely to create greater social division and economic inequality.

Conservative Ideology and Education

The policies being pursued by the present government are based on an ideology more appropriate to the nineteenth than the twenty-first century. Their vision is one of a nineteenth-century liberal individualism in which ostensibly free consumers embrace the laws of the market, and values of self-interest and personal and familial profit. It is supplemented by a traditional, conservative appeal to a nineteenth-century moral authoritarianism and a nostalgic imperialism in which individuals accept an hierarchical understanding of their class, gender, and 'racial' position and behave accordingly. Fairness and justice are not visible attributes.

The vision translates into an economic market doctrine driven by the belief that a precondition for consumer choice is the dismantling of a democratically controlled education system and its replacement by individual competitive schools with centrally controlled funding and curriculum.

The political importance attached to what is still a small part of the school system is evident in the continuous references to grant-maintained status in the government White paper *Choice and Diversity* (DFE 1992) and in the 1993 Education Act. It is clear that the government wishes the disappearance of local education authorities and intends this to happen via the centralisation or nationalisation of schools. A leader in *The Times* noted in July 1992 that 'it is extraordinary that a Conservative government should have such contempt for...the bands that tie schools to their communities through local democracy' and...'such faith in the rectitude of Whitehall planning'. Institutional and individual self-interest is the

3

ideology fuelling the 1993 Act. Government policy is driven by faith in supposed beneficial outcomes of market forces in which the weakest do not survive. In setting school against school the ideology takes no account of arguments that competition between schools actually contradicts the values most schools seek to uphold, and no account of evidence that such competition is likely to be detrimental to those already disadvantaged by the circumstances in which they live. The government White Paper resurrects the tired cliché that there will be 'parity of esteem' between different schools in order to offer 'choice', ignoring the history of English education and the reality that markets do not flourish in conditions of parity between products!

Within Conservative ideology education is a commodity with parents supposedly free to 'choose' the quality, location and amount. The best quality education is a positional good which must be rationed and competitively sought after. Values of competitive individualism, separation and exclusion are extolled and knowledge is itself regarded as a commodity for private consumption. The knowledge itself, however, must be carefully regulated and determined by the central government and is, within this vision, largely based on a late nineteenth-century curriculum with distinct cultural barriers between academic, practical, and technical learning. The social class origins of individuals are still largely intended to determine the kinds and amounts of knowledge 'consumed'. Indeed, education remains a preparation for a class-divided hierarchical society, still permeated (despite some introduction of technological and business studies and a rhetoric of national vocational qualifications) by an anti-technological and anti-industrial ethos, in which both skilled workers and those destined for places on the margins of the economy receive a different and inferior education to those who seek secure professional jobs and positions of influence in the society.

This ideology, and its developing educational framework and content, is narrow, backward-looking, and potentially disastrous in both economic and social terms for young British people about to move into the twenty-first century.

An Alternative Vision

An alternative model embraces the future, and must be appropriate to the twenty-first century, not a nostalgic yearning for the nineteenth.

Children starting school in the 1990s will live to the year 2070 and beyond. They deserve a new vision. Such a vision must, however, borrow 'eternal truisms' from the past, especially the realisation that 'no man is an island'. Humans are not simply egotistical beings satisfying private wants. They are also social and communal beings, bound to each other by obligations which transcend their private interests and are grounded in social good.

The new vision must be built on the notion of genuine democracy and transcend individualism, recognising that individuals can and must come together as a society. They can and must engage in public debate over economic, social and political arrangements if they want to reconstruct the values, beliefs and practices of their society. The system of education will express and create the values and framework of an educated democracy.

Such a system must be truly public, being more than the sum of individual choices, transcending crude class-based opportunism that competitively seeks education to gain and sustain privilege. It must be more than a set of schools competing with each other in an atmosphere of suspicion and image-presentation which destroys co-operation and collegiality. It must embrace the optimistic beliefs and values of a more equal, co-operative society, with fewer invidious distinctions and a determination to do away with gross material, social and educational inequities. The question: 'what is education for?' must no longer be answered by: 'to give me and/or my children advantages at the expense of others'.

This vision will not be easy to achieve. It will need an enormous shift in thinking to accept that there is literally 'no future' in continuing to ration good education in order to reproduce advantages for privileged groups. We are living through the creation of a post-industrial society in which we know that few unskilled and semi-skilled jobs will survive. The 'operative' (working) class will need the same knowledge and skills as the ruling and professional classes.

Education for the Future

John Sayer, in a recent book on the future governance of education (1993), has noted that while we are at the beginning of an analysis of the consequences of educational reforms, we can continue to take at face value claims that markets, choice and diversity are all about raising standards, and demonstrate that one does not automatically follow the other. We need evidence, so far not forthcoming, that the reforms actively are 'raising standards' for *all* children. We should not however neglect to ask the basic questions which have been ignored. What is the Conservative view of the society of the future and how does education reflect or project this view? (Sayer 1993, p.1) Is education to be solely designed to serve the improvement of material living standards via enhanced (post) industrial development at the expense of a quality of life less dependent on material goods? Is education about enhancing wealth-creating skills or skills for living without waste and destruction? Is it to be concerned with public provision for the needs of the individual, or private acquisition that is ultimately self-defeating?

Whatever the answers to these questions we do know that in the society of the future all young people will need to be able to solve problems (including some not yet imagined), to think for themselves, to engage in lifetime learning, to work in co-operation with others and to participate in the 'knowledge society' which has long been forecast, and is now upon us.

Reich, in his book *The Work of Nations* (1991) described the education of the future as one in which the skills of abstraction, system thinking, experimentation, and collaboration will be needed by all. He points out that while industrial economies only needed around 5 per cent of the population educated in this way, in the future 80 per cent of the workforce will need these skills.

The assumptions on which we base our current policies—that only 20 to 30 per cent of the population need be academic and technical elites, with 70 per cent receiving a minimalist education and low-skill training—are wildly wide of the mark. An untrained population cannot understand what it is doing, and how it might adapt to new technologies, while still creating humanistic environments.

Those who participate in 'work' of any kind (and in the twenty-first century people will move in and out of 'work', change employment, engage in life-long learning) will need to overcome reluctance to master ideas and skills, and develop new attitudes to thinking, learning, and intellectual 'work' in general. Those who participate in leisure and recreational activities and in family and social life will also need new skills, ideas and understanding.

As citizens, people will need much more preparation to be aware of the complexity of their rights and obligations, and parents will need to acquire more conscious skills as they accept a more equal partnership with teachers in the education of the next generation. All citizens of nation-states will need to be more aware of the 'global society', and the interdependence of nations, the perils of ethnic nationalism, and the translation of old imperialisms into positive help for developing nations.

In the twenty-first century the survival of the human species itself will depend on self-restraint and co-operation, with a more highly developed sense of personal, social and moral responsibility as a prerequisite for each individual. This is the opposite of neo-conservative calls for a return to a moral authority in which people know their place. The value system of society will need to change from amoral values encouraged by primitive and competitive market operations and selfish class-based interests.

New Principles for a New Vision

The principles on which this new vision could be based will need careful working out. One principle would be that education is not a commodity to be bought, sold or rationed in market transactions. It is a right and a precondition of freedom for all citizens. It involves an opening up to knowledge, ways of understanding and the development of abilities which create informed, caring and co-operative citizens. It offers the development of intellectual capacities, economic skills, and personal qualities that every individual has the right to acquire and the obligation to put to the service of society.

A second principle will be that education offers the promise of freedom—three freedoms 'from' and five freedoms 'to'. These are: freedom from ignorance; freedom from economic want; freedom from political, social and economic manipulation. The others are freedom to develop intellectual and practical capacities; to put talents and capacities to the service of society; to exercise critical and informed judgements; to develop understanding and personal integrity; to respect fellow humans and associates in a community of equals.

Quality in education and 'raised standards' will depend on a commitment from all those involved working to achieve a common vision. It will depend on teachers having high expectations of all children, pupils and students having a high motivation to learn, civil servants and administrators having a commitment to the fair allocation

7

of resources. On international comparisons the top 20 per cent of attainers achieve as well as any other country, but for the rest achievements in education and training compare unfavourably (Green and Steedman 1993). Quality and equality go hand-in-hand: quality education for all does demand fair resourcing, and does not, for example, single out grant-maintained schools, CTCs or shire counties for preferential funding. There is no dilemma between excellence and equity in education if the principle of quality education for all informs policy.

Conclusion

The papers presented to the Ibis Hotel Seminar indicated that a market in education cannot ensure fair provision for all young people in the society. Research carried out on some of the government's educational reforms to date indicates that the enormous upheavals in every aspect of the education service are not leading to improved education for all, raised standards or fair resourcing. What appears to be happening is that a larger elite is receiving a well-resourced and improved education at the expense of the majority, and there is little evidence to date that a better educated and skilled workforce is being created. In addition, the reforms have begun to erode local democracy, centralise power in the hands of the Secretary of State for Education, redistribute resources towards and expand choice for middle-class students, while moving resources and choice away from working-class students and those with disadvantages and learning difficulties. They have emasculated a respected inspectorate, and failed to produce coherent post-16 policies. Alternative educational policies should be based on research findings, should be coherent and rational, and should re-affirm the right of every person to have access to the best education that can be provided. The reforms and the ideology on which they are based offer false promises of choice, 'classlessness' and freedom. The language of conservatism and the workings of an educational market will produce neither virtuous citizens nor successful entrepreneurs. This obsolete vision continues to encourage the selection of those already advantaged for more privileged schooling and reinforces the divisions and failures of education in the twentieth century.

The new model offers the framework and value of an educated democracy in which good education ceases to be a competitive prize and becomes the basis for an economic, political and cultural order from which no one is excluded. The prize becomes a more humane and defensible view of individuals and their capacity to join together as a human society.

PART 1
COMPETITIVE SYSTEMS

1 MARKET FORCES AND PARENTAL CHOICE: SELF-INTEREST AND COMPETITIVE ADVANTAGE IN EDUCATION

Stephen J. Ball, Richard Bowe and Sharon Gewirtz

The market solution to most matters currently holds politicians around the world in its thrall. We should not be surprised by this for the market provides politicians with all the benefits of being seen to act decisively and very few of the problems of being blamed when things go wrong. Because, so the theory goes, the market is a mechanism which produces its own order. Responsibility is devolved to the individual consumer and the aggregate of consumer choices provides the discipline, of accountability and demand, that the producer cannot escape. The energetic and careful are rewarded and the slothful and ignorant are punished. If things go wrong then misguided consumers or tardy producers are to blame, not the politician. The market appears to be a hands-off policy. And if we have faith in the market and its order, we also know (are supposed to believe) that things will turn out all right in the end, even if there is a degree of creative destruction along the way. The forces of the market will out, the good will survive, the weak will go to the wall, and everyone will be better off than before if not equally well off—an absence of inequality in the marketplace means an absence of striving and competition. The market system is driven by self-interest: the self-interest of the consumer, the parent choosing a school that will provide maximum advantage to their child, and the self-interest of the producer, the school, or its senior managers, in making policy decisions that are based upon ensuring that their institution thrives, or at least survives, in the marketplace. Thus, in areas where there are surplus places and schools are in competition with one another for student recruitment, rivalry and emulation become key elements of the relationships between schools. The demand for school places is inelastic, the number of potential students is fixed. Survival can only be ensured by attracting consumers away from other schools. In areas where there is little or no surplus capacity, the onus of competition switches to parents. Within all this, one of the things brought about by the introduction of the market system is the 'privatisation' of significant aspects of education policy.

Education, in this respect, is being transformed from a public to a private good. The local provision of educational services is no longer planned in relation to 'need' but is left to family choices and management decision-making. These are the bases of the 'natural' order, the 'hidden hand' of market forces. However, in practice in the UK, the school market is not entirely unplanned nor entirely natural. It is focused, framed and influenced by the political objectives of the Conservative government. The government retains control of and imposes a system of performance indicators upon the education market (through National Tests and the publication of league tables etc.). These are intended, in one respect, to provide the system of information and knowledge which is so important in any market, in allowing consumers to make 'best' choices. But they also orient the provision of education towards certain goals and purposes, as discussed below, and create particular patterns of self-interest for schools which systematically disadvantage certain groups of students.

In any attempt to review the workings of the education market, it is important to note the political tensions and contradictions which underlie its operation. On the one hand, the pursuit of the ideology of the market from the 1993 Education Act is intended to develop increased diversity among schools. But this diversity is still to be set within the centrally determined National Curriculum and is in no way clearly related to consumer preferences. It is a further example of planned political intervention into the market. On the other hand, the 1993 Act indicates a commitment to reduce surplus places in the school system (estimated to be around 900,000). This reduction in places, driven by a concern to cut overall educational expenditure by reducing unit costs, would reduce the competitive edge in the education market, give greater power in the marketplace to the producers and further reduce the 'realities' of choice for many parents. (It is worth noting here the different conceptions and calculations of surplus places employed in this debate between the ideology of choice and unit costs. The DFE and LEAs, in their funding of schools and setting of standard numbers, work with a calculation different from the Audit Commission. The latter relates surplus places to capacity: that is, the maximum number of students that each school could physically cope with. In the system currently operating some schools are oversubscribed, that is 'full' to their standard number but working under 'capacity'. Others are undersubscribed but over capacity.) Set against all this, the provisions of the 1993 Act, which will allow the possibility of the setting up of new schools, will increase surplus places and unit costs, unless existing schools are also closed. The politics, ideology and economics of the education market are each in contradiction with the other.

It also needs to be said that choice is only real for some parents in some places. Not all parents are able or willing to avail themselves of the possibilities of or cope with the complexities of choice (see below). And in many areas of the country there is no possibility of choice. The rise in the number of appeals and in the number of disgruntled consumers who find they have no choice indicates the mismatch between ideology and practicality.

Education currently provides one of several natural laboratories in the public sector in which the market experiment is being tried out. Here we want to reflect on some early evidence and medium-term thoughts derived from an ESRC-funded study of 'Market Forces in Education' conducted at the Centre for Educational Studies, King's College, London, 1991–4. The study is focused upon a set of specific education markets over a 39-month period. Three clusters of second-ary schools in three adjacent LEAs were identified as sites of local competition—15 schools in all, including LEA and grant main-tained, mixed and single sex, two church schools and a CTC. The LEAs are very different in terms of social class and ethnic mix and each has a different majority party in control of the local council. Each has a different orientation to and engagement with the education market. These sites were chosen not for any reasons of representative-ness but because competititon between schools was possible and likely. First of all, we have been monitoring the market behaviour of the schools—attending meetings, collecting documents, visiting open evenings and interviewing a cross-section of staff and governors in each. We have been interested in how the schools seek to attract parents, their responsiveness to market 'signals', as well as their relationships with one another and with their LEA. Second, in each of the three years of the study we have conducted interviews with a sample of parents in each of the clusters—approximately 150 in all. The sample has been designed roughly to match the class and ethnic composition of the cluster localities. The interviews—most with mothers—are conducted in some depth, and parents are asked to talk about the processes of 'choice', reasons, constraints, sources of information, influences, decision-making, etc. We have not simply been eliciting criteria; indeed we find that the focus on criteria of choice, which dominates much of the existing research, can be profoundly misleading, and further we have not assumed that choice is relevant and meaningful for all parents. We contacted parents of year 6 students through primary schools and the interviews were conducted during the period of 'choosing' in order to capture the flux of choice-making rather than record post-factum reconstructions and legitimations. We were also able to interview a number of primary headteachers. Third, we have been collecting, from the LEAs, where possible, data on the overall pattern of choices for secondary schools in order to plot changes over time in the 'popularity' of schools and to identify any changes in the social and spatial distribution of access to schools. However, as the mechanisms of primary/secondary transfer become increasingly deregulated the collection of such data becomes more difficult. The research is intended to move beyond the study of parental choice and school responsiveness in isolation to begin to make some sense of the overall dynamics of local markets.

The following section outlines the points arising from our research, each of which adumbrates a market 'effect'.

☐ one of the key premises upon which our research rests is that education markets are essentially localised and that, despite some common features, local markets will differ from one another by virtue of their histories, their local government, their spatial organisation and transport infrastructure and the socio-economic structure of the local communities they serve. Local markets in education are complex and idiosyncratic. (In contrast to the platitudinous simplicities offered in government policy documents and ministerial statements.) They have their own dynamic, structures and history.

☐ none of the fifteen secondary schools involved in our study can afford to ignore the marketplace. While some are better placed than others, being oversubscribed, there is an awareness that there is a degree of volatility and fashion in parental choice. And the system of year-on-year funding of schools encourages this sense of anxiety. In our interviews with headteachers the need 'not to be complacent' was pointed up by everyone. The discipline of the market bites. Nonetheless, the logic of the market suggests that those schools which are oversubscribed or working more or less at full capacity have less reason to change what they are currently doing, or at least radically to rethink their current practice, than those schools currently significantly undersubscribed. They are, in general terms at least, satisfying

16

their consumers. However, our research clearly indicates that it is a mistake to see patterns of choice as being solely an expression of educational preference in any simple sense. There is no *simple* relationship between enrolment and quality, as some advocates of choice would have us believe. What might be called the 'accidents' of the market, as well as the effects of 'market planning', bring extraneous factors into play. Examples of the first are geography and demography—some 'good' schools are difficult to get to or serve declining populations. An example of the second is the opening of a new school adjacent to an old, with the effect of diverting enrolments. Furthermore, it is not clear that schools in the marketplace are oriented to or responsive to either the needs or wants of parents in any *simple* sense.

☐ schools are paying a lot more attention to what parents want for their children's education. Or more precisely what schools *think* that parents want. Or even more precisely what schools think that *some* parents want. In a few cases schools are engaging in crude forms of 'market research' or are consulting public relations firms but for the most part the 'responsiveness' of schools is based upon impressions or the emulation of rivals. (All of this still begs the question as to whether parents always know what is best educationally for their children.)

☐ the publication of examination league tables and other performance indicators has meant that schools are increasingly keen to attract enrolments from 'motivated' parents and 'able' children who are likely to enhance their relative position in local systems of competition. In a sense there is a shift of emphasis from student needs to student performance: from what the school can do for the student to what the student can do for the school.

☐ in relation to the above there is increasing evidence of a shift of resources away from students with special needs and learning difficulties. Well established and proven systems of SEN teaching in schools are being dismantled or much reduced in size. Resources are being directed more towards those students who are most likely to perform well in tests and examinations. The reintroduction of setting and streaming proceeds apace. (This is also driven by the introduction of differentiated syllabuses for GCSE and parts of the National Curriculum.)

☐ generally the role of SEN work in schools is being played down. Schools which have histories of excellence in SEN work are concerned that they will become labelled by parents as 'caring' rather than 'academic' institutions. In some cases schools which have attracted large numbers of statemented students are trying to reorient their recruitment efforts to attract different sorts of students. One rather sad and dramatic comment from an SEN teacher illustrates the climate of concern now in place in the education market.

> We don't want to become a secondary modern, especially anyway if the special needs department is so understaffed anyway. We can't cope with the numbers of students that need the help....Next year, for instance, we're having a kid who's got Down's Syndrome. He's going to be joining us and then there was another one with another, not Down's but something else who also thought, ah yes, Northwark Park and we thought, well no, we can't take two. This is going to be enough having one child with that level of need and integrating. I mean it's such a new thing for us, we can't deal with two, we just can't handle it, we're going to be stretched enough as it is, but luckily the parents have decided to go elsewhere....But we were beginning to think, oh my gosh, are we going to start getting a reputation, ah yes, Northwark Park, they integrate students with these difficulties and then, you know, what effect does that have on the perception of parents with that school, when they come to want a school for their band one kid, do they send them to that school?

☐ some of the money and energy previously devoted to educational endeavours like SEN work are now focused upon marketing activities. Most schools have some kind of marketing or public relations committee. Brochures and prospectuses are glossier and more carefully thought out; logos, uniforms, headed letter paper, etc. are being planned to create a corporate image aimed at potential consumers. In some instances Public Relations firms are bought in. The skills and knowledge of some school governors can also be important in these areas. Open evenings, items in the local press, newspaper advertising and school performances are now part of marketing strategy. In some of our research schools staff are under pressure to change their style of dress to give a 'better' impression to parents. Hype, image and impression management are very much to the fore.

☐ all of the above are of course related to competition, to rivalry among local schools for student recruitment. Where there are large numbers of surplus places then the competition is intense and the 'responses' outlined above are clearer. Where places are filled or where there are no nearby rivals then the competition and the 'response' effects are more muted. In metropolitan areas where competition is at its most cut-throat previous systems of co-operation and collaboration among schools have been severely curtailed and replaced by a climate of suspicion and hostility. Headteachers are beginning to talk about 'poaching', 'industrial espionage', 'knocking copy' and 'underhand moves'—always on the part of other schools, of course. Significantly, as already noted, if the intention signalled in the 1993 Education Act to reduce surplus places is carried through, then both the numbers of successful choices and the pressure of competition among schools will be reduced.

☐ the changes above amount to a significant shift in the value framework of education. In the market, shrewdness rather than principles is rewarded. Long-held commitments and beliefs are being abandoned or compromised in order to ensure institutional survival. Commercial rather than educational principles are increasingly dominant in making curriculum and organisation and resource decisions.

☐ part of this value shift is evident in the 'gap' which is opening up between the management and teachers of schools, one of values, purposes and concerns. Management is increasingly dominated by issues of marketing and recruitment, finance and budgeting. Teaching is dominated by delivery of the National Curriculum and sometimes at least the educational needs of individual students. The culture of school management is steadily becoming divorced from educational concerns. As one deputy head in the research explained: 'the senior management team are no longer managing education but managing an educational institution'.

☐ on the other side of the market, the consumer side, some parents are clearly becoming more active in exercising the possibilities of choice (where available). Middle-class parents in particular are exploiting the market in education and bringing their social and cultural advantages to bear. In general terms the education market is more geared to the consumption values and modes of the middle classes. Middle-class parents are more likely to have the knowledge, skills and contacts to decode and manipulate what are increasingly complex and deregulated systems of choice and recruitment. The more deregulation, the more possibility of informal procedures being employed. The middle classes also, on the whole, are more able and willing to move their children around the system.

☐ by contrast we find that working-class parents are more likely to prefer *the* local school for their children. This in part reflects a more limited knowledge of other schools and the economic and familial constraints within which choice of school is set. School has to be 'fitted' into a set of limitations and expectations related to work roles, family roles, the sexual division of labour and the demands of household organisation. And the material and cultural aspects of this are difficult to separate. For our middle-class respondents it was much more common to find family roles and household organisation being accommodated to school. But it is not simply a matter of education being of less importance for working-class families; our interviewees were very concerned that their children should receive a good education. Rather, the competing pressures of work and family life made certain possibilities difficult or impossible to contemplate and others seem obvious and appropriate. Choice of school was 'embedded' in a complex pattern of family demands and structural limitations. This is not a matter of cultural deficit but rather pragmatic accommodation. *But locality is also a positive value for many working-class parents.* They want their children to go to a school which is easily accessible and does not involve long and dangerous journeys; a school where friends', neighbours' and relatives' children also go; a school which is a part of their social community, their locality.

☐ one way of making some sense of the differences in market participation among parents is to consider participation in relation to inclination and capacity. Inclination entails the wish to maximise one's child's interests in the marketplace. It rests on a belief that schools vary in terms, for instance, of atmosphere, the 'standard of education' they offer, their exam results, the life chances they facilitate, the values they impart, the extent of extra-curricular activities, the kind of children that go to them, levels of resourcing, levels of parental support, and the commitment of teachers. Because schools are seen to vary, the market-oriented parent feels that it is necessary to examine what is on offer in order to seek out the best or at least avoid the worst. (This does not imply a single and unequivocal hierarchy of schools but a view, held by some parents, that a particular sort of school is most appropriate for or in the best interests of their child.)

☐ the inclination towards consumerism is underpinned by a certain degree of self-confidence. The consumerist parent feels able to distinguish—at least in certain respects—between a 'good' school and a 'bad' school. Confidence is one aspect of the package of cultural resources which enable some parents to operate the market to their children's advantage. Thus inclination to play the market and capacity to do so are in some ways interlinked. However, there are many parents who have the inclination to engage with the market, but who do not have the capacity to 'work' the market effectively. These are the parents who are frustrated in the marketplace.

□ capacity is enhanced both by material resources and the right kind of cultural capital. Material resources confer a number of obvious advantages in the educational market place: (1) They maximise opportunities for transport. The range of schools to choose from is more extensive for parents who can afford to pay for long journeys on public transport or who can use private cars or taxis for awkward routes. Although LEAs provide the financially disadvantaged with free passes, these are not generally valid for travel to out-LEA schools. It is also often the case that middle-class areas tend to be better served by public transport; (2) They allow greater flexibility for moving house and thus greatly extended choice of school, that is 'selection by mortgage' continues to operate; (3) They enable coaching for grammar and private school entrance exams as well as payment of school fees and so give greater access to selective schools; (4) Child care opportunities are enhanced so that where parents have more than one child, they can send their children to schools at a distance from one another. Conversely those who lack material resources and work full-time can be severely hampered by their child care arrangements because they have to rely on older children to collect the younger ones from school and care for them afterwards. These parents are 'time poor'. Greater access to child care also facilitates more extensive consumerist activity. Open evenings and days at secondary schools tend to be organised over a two- or three-week period in the autumn term. A number of parents commented on how exhausting the intensive visiting of schools over a short time is. With young children in tow it is especially draining. Single parents who do not have anyone with whom to share child care responsibilities and who cannot afford baby sitters are particularly limited in how much browsing they can do when it comes to choosing a school. In addition, middle-class jobs tend to provide greater flexibility for timetable juggling, so that, for example, if an evening visit is inconvenient, time can be made during the day to visit a school. All of these small inequalities contribute to significantly different patterns of participation and opportunity.

□ whilst material resources greatly enhance choice, having a certain degree of cultural capital 'in the right currency' is indispensable for playing the market successfully. Having the right kind of cultural capital means being knowledgable about and familiar with the education system and having the confidence to 'work' it. Those who have always 'done well' out of the system themselves—that is, those who have had a 'good education', got 'good jobs' etc., tend to have more confidence in negotiating it. 'Working the system' involves knowing which strategies to use to maximise one's chances of getting a good deal out of it. Examples of such strategies from our own interviews include attempting to make an impression with the headteacher at the open day, making a private appointment to visit the headteacher, knowing how to mount a successful appeal, and, most commonly, putting in multiple applications. Those who work inside the system—teachers, education administrators, governors—are particularly well endowed with the right sort of cultural capital. Because they work in the system they feel more able to distinguish between presentational veneer and educational substance and tend to be more cynical about marketing. Insiders are likely to be more aware of the complexities of choosing, the arbitrariness of the choice process, the difficulties of using exam results as indicators of good schools, how to 'read' exam results, and of how the appeal system works.

☐ playing the market demands a great deal of stamina—to research, visit schools, make multiple applications and appeal—and that stamina is sustained by knowledge, contacts, time and money. Whilst 'insiders' are particularly privileged in the marketplace, 'outsiders' are particularly disadvantaged. The latter might include those who went to schools in other countries and so are not familiar with the system, those who do not feel confident enough about their English language skills to be able to negotiate the system or who do not have the necessary contacts to assist them in working it. Their cultural capital is in the wrong currency and they are less able to accumulate the right sort. Whilst such parents might be inclined to play the market, they are poorly equipped to do so effectively.

☐ social class (and in some respects ethnicity and gender) is a key factor in the dynamics of the market in another sense. There are indications in our research data of relationships between certain class fractions and preference for certain styles and ethos of schooling. The class and ethnic composition of schools is also for some parents a criterion in their selection of schools. Social class is a factor in the 'niche' market attractions of certain schools. Some parents are particularly concerned about who their child will go to school with.

☐ the changes in school policies indicated earlier involve a shift in the range of choices now available to parents. Certain choices are being privileged. Parents who want a comprehensive school (using that term to represent a paradigm for a particular set of values and practices), may find their choice being squeezed out of the marketplace. Parents with children with special educational needs will also find that some schools will give preference to other less expensive and less demanding children. In political rhetoric the differences between choosing (making a choice) and getting your choice are systematically ignored. More specialisation and selection will mean more and more frustrated choosers.

☐ paradoxically, and despite the former Education Minister John Patten's enthusiasm for specialisation, one effect of emulation and rivalry (and of the system of published performance indicators) was a greater 'dull uniformity' among schools as they sought to play safe, emulate 'popular' rivals and compete for the same desirable students.

☐ insofar as students are influenced and affected by the hidden curriculum of their institutional environment then the system of morality 'taught' by schools is increasingly well accommodated to the values complex of the enterprise culture. All of this is particularly ironic (or maybe not) given the espoused commitment of the UK government to the development of 'a moral dimension' in schools (DFE White Paper, *Choice and Diversity*, 1992 para. 1.29, p.7). Caught between the state and the market the school may be on the way to becoming a reflection of and playing its part in reproducing what Kingdom (Kingdom 1992) calls the 'masturbatory society'; 'offering a solitary view of fulfilment, free of the complications arising from tiresome moral demands by others' (p.1).

☐ in substantive terms, within the UK education system there is now a struggle underway over values. We suggest that, at least in recent years, the values of comprehensivism have constituted and provided a language and ethic of civic virtue in education. These are now being destroyed by and replaced by market values. Comprehensive values (Daunt 1975) are essentially an articulation of Nagel's 'impersonal standpoint' and can be contrasted along several dimensions with the 'culture of self interest' or 'personal standpoint' represented in market values (Nagel 1991). As a 'moral tradition' comprehensivism provides a framework for ethical concerns; it articulates a way of life based upon communitarian principles. It provides for a 'thick' morality— shared values and common sentiments. This falls within what Lowery et al. call the 'public sphere', a space in our social world in which issues are open to debate, reflection and moral argument (Lowery et al. 1992). The market, by contrast, rests on aggregative principles, the sum of individual goods and choices, 'founded on individual and property rights that enable citizens to address problems of interdependence via exchange' (ibid.). It provides for a 'thin' morality and generates hierarchy and division based upon competitive individualism.

All of the above taken together leave us with some difficult questions to answer as to how we should understand the education market and parental choice theoretically. We find recent theories of consumption a useful starting point here (Featherstone 1992). Clearly, it would be a mistake to treat the processes and relations revealed here simply in abstract terms as 'economic'. In any case the economy only exists in this pure and abstract way in the imaginations of economists. 'The economic' is variously present in a whole variety of situations that individuals and institutions face. One way of talking about this would be in terms of individuals' 'problematics', which we might loosely define as their continued negotiation of the various aspects of their lives making use of the resources (following Bourdieu, their different species of capital) that they are able to bring to bear. Such problematics are contextualised by the way in which both institutional and systemic values and processes cut across individuals' lives. Institutions, in turn, could be viewed as having 'acquired' volumes of capital (an historical dimension) that then allow them stronger power positions than individuals and make them prime sites for struggle to possess this 'institutionalised' capital which may be used for different purposes. 'Consumption' is not the obverse of production, or vice versa: each is embedded in the situations and aspirations of active agents who are able, to different degrees, to appropriate the forms of capital that circulate within these processes. To focus only on 'the act of consumption' or 'the culture of consumption' is to draw our attention away from the profoundly social nature of the process.

We would suggest that 'embedding' agents in their social milieu requires careful, ethnographically based analyses that produce a 'more socialised' view of the educational process (Kemeny 1992). Rather than assuming that class and class fractions provide an adequate characterisation of how one lives, perhaps we need to consider the varied ways in which people are socially embedded. That does not mean excluding or replacing class analysis but instead recognising that 'new hierarchies and differentiations develop which are internal to social class' (Beck 1992, p. 97.) In Beck's analysis of the transition to what he terms flexible modernisation he suggests that,

The individual is indeed removed from the traditional
commitments and support relationships, but exchanges them for
the constraints of existence in the labour market and as a
consumer, with the standardizations and controls they contain.
(Beck 1992, p.131)

He indicates the need to analyse this transition as part of the process
of individualisation that has characterised social change since at least
the early 1950s. Both situations in life (objective) and consciousness
and identity (subjective) are implicated in these processes. This
suggests that we need to reconsider how we conceptualise a concept
such as class; not abandon it. Thus, in looking at micro-markets our
analyses have taken a critical approach to the use of the concept of
class and we have used both categorical (Ball, Gewirtz and Bowe
1994) and typological differences (Gewirtz, Ball and Bowe 1993) in
order to explore class. We envisage that the continued investigation of
how parental embeddedness in a variety of social contexts informs the
processes of school transfer will lead to further critical assessment of
how we employ concepts such as class, race and gender. Models of
consumption do help to broaden our conception of the 'social' and it
seems to us that if the sociology of education is to make progress in
grasping the nature of social and educational change, then it must
engage with critical appraisals, theoretical reworkings and new
directions in social theory.

This is a very schematic summary of some of the trends and issues
emerging from our research. Many of the issues are a great deal more
complex than we have been able to indicate here. But the disciplinary
effects of the market are clear, the patterns of advantage and
disadvantage are stark, and the value shifts are marked. Whether all of
this will lead to a raising of standards remains to be seen. It might,
but some people may want to ask 'at what cost?'. Let us conclude
starkly by asserting one of those costs. The education market reasserts,
reinforces and celebrates in a major way the opportunity advantages
of middle-class parents. Whatever muting of opportunity differences
and de-differentiating effects comprehensive schools have had these
are now in the process of thorough deconstruction by market forces.
As a result, we are likely to end up with a more socially differentiated
and divisive system of education. In any market there are winners and
losers. In this market we may all end up losing out!

2 UNDERPINNING CHOICE AND DIVERSITY? THE GRANT-MAINTAINED SCHOOLS POLICY IN CONTEXT

Sally Power, David Halpin and John Fitz

The 1988 Education Reform Act (ERA) allows schools to 'opt out' of local education authority (LEA) control and become 'grant-maintained' (GM). In common with much educational reform, the precise objectives of the GM schools policy are complex and shifting. Nevertheless, its advocates have consistently claimed that GM schools will encourage the growth of local education 'markets' through diversifying school provision and extending parental choice. They argue that by enabling schools to free themselves from the 'dead hand' of LEAs, opting out will break down the latter's monopoly on state schooling which has been perceived by New Right critics (e.g., Hillgate Group 1986, No Turning Back Group 1986 and Sexton 1989) to have contributed to a education system of mediocrity, homogeneity and inefficiency.

Opting out, however, represents only one of several policies aimed at restructuring education provision along market principles. Other initiatives, particularly the establishment of City Technology Colleges (CTCs), open enrolment, and the per capita funding formula entailed in the Local Management of Schools (LMS), are also explicitly designed to contribute to a system in which schools are increasingly forced to compete with each other for their pupils and thus become more accountable to parents. Even so, the continuing and central importance of opting out within government policy is evident in the White Paper *Choice and Diversity—a new framework for schools* which predicts, among other things, that:

> By the next century, we will have achieved a system characterised not by uniformity but by choice, underpinned by the spread of grant-maintained schools. (DFE 1992; p.64)

The subsequent 1993 Education Act contains a number of measures designed to stimulate opting out. These include simplification of the balloting procedures and limits on the amount an LEA can spend to campaign against opting out. In addition, governing bodies of LEA schools are now obliged to consider 'going GM' once in every school year.

At the time of writing, the continued promotion and expansion of the policy had led to nearly 1500 schools embarking on the process of opting out, of which 800 were operating as GM schools (DFE Progress Report, February 1993). Although the size of the GM sector has increased, there is little to suggest that the policy has fulfilled the objectives of its advocates. Drawing on empirical research into the early impact and experience of opting out, this paper contends that GM schools have yet to achieve diversity in educational provision or enhance parental choice. It argues, however, that the limited impact of opting out needs to be analysed not simply in terms of the deficiencies within the policy itself, but also in terms of the context in which it is implemented. The paper concludes by suggesting that it is only through enhanced understanding of contextual features that the limits and possibilities of future alternative education policies can be more fully comprehended.

Opting Out, Expanding Choice and Diversifying Provision

Advocates of the GM schools policy argue that GM status will lead not only to improvements within individual schools which opt out, but will also widen choice through creating a 'new' kind of school. In addition to 'challenging' other state schools to 'do better' (Baker 1987), GM schools, it is claimed, will break down the barrier between public and private provision. They will, in other words, become a 'half-way house' between state and independent schools, ending the existing dualism where 'only the wealthy have choice' (Tebbit 1987). It is important to remember that these measures are aimed at widening educational opportunity as much as 'raising standards'. And while competition, and therefore a degree of inequality is necessary for the operation of market dynamics, the government claims that diversification and specialisation will result in lateral differentiation of provision rather than the linear hierarchy which its critics anticipate. The government 'wants to ensure that there are no tiers of schools within the maintained system but parity of esteem between different schools' (DFE 1992, p.10).

Attempts to assess the impact of any policy are always complex, and often contested. Supporters of opting out argue that the increasing number of positive ballot results from schools seeking GM status and augmented subscription rates at schools which have opted out provide evidence that the policy is 'successful' (e.g., Rumbold 1990, Patten 1993). While not disputing that individual GM schools are popular with parents, our research does not indicate that, thus far, they are 'successful' in terms of diversifying provision and extending parental choice.

Our findings, derived from a larger study of opting out (Halpin and Fitz 1990; Fitz et al. 1993a), are based on semi-structured interviews with pupils and parents using eight GM schools (selected to represent the diversity of the secondary sector as a whole: rural and urban, inner-city and suburban, comprehensive and academically selective, single-sex and co-educational) and those using neighbouring LEA and independent schools in two areas. In total, 460 students (264 from eight GM schools, 124 from four LEA schools and 72 from two independent schools) and 216 of their parents were interviewed (for fuller details see Fitz et al. 1993b, Chapters 5 and 6).

The evaluation of dimensions of 'choice' is, of course, highly complex as it involves both subjective perception and material opportunity. We have found little evidence, however, to show that opting out has made any difference to either the directions along which parents and pupils choose schools or the nature of provision which is being made available to them. Certainly, few of our sample of parents who had selected a school after it had opted out felt that GM status had any bearing on their choice. Of those who did, the significance of 'going GM' was not usually perceived in terms of providing a 'new' choice, but of holding on to an 'old' one. There were some who made reference to aspects of GM status beyond increased security as being relevant to their choice. But for all those who saw the school's new status as a bonus factor, there were as many who claimed to have selected a GM school *despite* it having opted out.

Perhaps the lack of reference to the official designation of a school is unsurprising given the criteria and sources of information upon which most school choices are made. Our data, like that of others (e.g., West et al. 1993, Webster 1993), indicate that nearly all the parents, irrespective of the kind of school their children attended, made their decision largely on the basis of locally constructed accounts of 'reputation' and 'atmosphere'. Furthermore, given that the GM schools in our sample were incorporated for only a few terms, most of the informal accounts and family/friend connections stem from their *pre*-GM status. Accordingly, the local confidence expressed through the popularity of a GM school appears to be founded less on the school's new status, but rather more on the preservation and continuity of its recent past.

The extent to which GM status represents continuity is evident in the experiences of the pupils who attend GM schools. Although the degree of awareness varies from school to school, it is noteworthy that of all our sample, one quarter were completely unaware that their school had undergone any change in status and were quite unacquainted with what 'grant-maintained' might mean. This is not to say that they had not noticed any changes. In every GM school, pupils made reference to redecoration and refurbishment of the school's buildings and the arrival of new resources subsequent upon incorporation. In addition, in all but one of our sample GM schools, pupils made unprompted comment on the extent to which school rules in general, and dress codes in particular, were being more vigorously reinforced. Beyond the extra funding and renewed traditional imagery, there were, however, no indications of any changes relating to the curriculum or pedagogy. Therefore, it would appear that, for most pupils, GM status is not perceived as marking a transition, let alone a transformation.

That GM status tends to preserve existing options rather than provide new alternatives is further endorsed through parents' perceptions about the range and nature of choices available to them. For instance, while most of those parents who claimed they had 'no choice' were those using local authority schools (see Table 2.1), for both the sample as a whole, and within particular sectors, there was little difference in the perceived range and availability of 'choice' either before or after their child's school, or neighbouring school, had opted out. In one area which we studied, there was an increase in the proportion of parents using the selective GM schools who claimed they had a wider choice of schools opting out, and a corresponding decrease in the range of choices which the LEA parents perceived as available. Such a pattern can be explained through the strengthening of the academic selection procedures subsequent to opting out, rather than stemming from GM status on its own. It certainly does not indicate a widening of choice for *all* parents in the area. That GM status, by itself, does not alter perceptions of available choice is

Table 2.1   Parents' perception of availability of choice

	'Some choice'	*'No choice'*
'GM' parents (N = 106)	71%	26%
'LEA' parents (N = 56)	57%	39%

evident from another of our study areas where admissions policies remained unaffected. Here, there was little change in the number of parents claiming to have 'choice', either before or after opting out.

Another indicator of the effects of GM status on parental choice is comparison of the frequency with which parents achieved a place at the school of their 'first choice'. Ninety per cent of our sample of parents claimed they were successful in realising their first choice. There were, however, notable variations within the sample. All of our independent parents said they achieved a place at the school of their choice, as did 93 per cent of GM parents, whereas this was the case for only 79 per cent of LEA parents. Such figures might indicate that GM schools are perceived as more desirable than their LEA counterparts. As with the data on perceptions of choice, such general cross-sector comparisons have many weaknesses, for choice is articulated within the circumstances of specific, local contexts. Indeed, there are marked variations within each sector. While the *average* first choice incidence is higher within the GM sector, individual LEA schools score both higher and lower. And even where 'first choice' incidence is higher in a school that has opted out, such popularity is not unambiguously connected with GM status. In particular, differences in first choice realisation appear, again, to be mainly connected with selective schooling where GM status has resulted in higher academic admission criteria. Here, increased first choice realisation by parents of 'successful' candidates is matched by increasing rates of disappointment by those who fail the entrance examinations. In any event, comparison of 'first choice' incidence before and after incorporation reveals a drop in frequency across *both* state sectors (see Table 2.2). Either way, the most that one can say is that GM status consolidates existing patterns of first choice preference, particularly where it coincides with selective schooling, rather than alters relative positions either between sectors or between individual schools.

Neither have we found anything to suggest that GM schools have, as yet, contributed to enhanced opportunities for those parents and children who were previously 'denied' choice. There is certainly little

Table 2.2 First choice realisation across sectors

	First choice realisation	
	Pre-GM (N = 75)	Post-GM (N = 107)
GM schools	95%	92%
LEA schools	88%	75%
Independent schools	100%	100%

evidence, for instance, that opted out schools have been able to blur the boundary between state and private schooling. For our sample, there was no change in the proportion of parents using state schools who had 'looked' to the independent sector before and after opting out. Similarly, parents using independent schools were no more likely to have considered a GM school than any state-maintained school. Qualitative data on pupil perceptions also suggest that the gulf between 'state' and 'private' is as wide as ever.

Just as our sample of GM schools cannot be said to have provided a 'half-way house' between state and private provision, so too have they had little impact on patterns of school choice and social class. Comparison of the social class compositions of schools (using the Hope-Goldthorpe classification [Goldthorpe and Hope 1974]) reveals that, although there are significant differences between schools, these have altered little since opting out. While it is the case that in both the areas we studied closely, the occupational profile of parents using the GM schools exhibits a high representation of service and intermediate classes, this does not indicate that GM schools have become the dominant type of school for middle-class parents. 'Popular' LEA schools were able to attract parents whose socio-economic status is as high, if not higher, than the neighbouring GM school. Nor has there been any significant shift in the social composition of our study schools subsequent to opting out.

Although such data might allay the fears of those who believe that opting out will lead to a new hierarchy of institutions (e.g., Walford and Miller 1991) reflecting and reinforcing existing patterns of socio-economic stratification (Edwards and Whitty 1992), it does nothing to support the claims of the policy's advocates that GM schools will widen opportunity. In both our study areas, the two schools with the lowest first choice incidence are also those located in working-class districts, and used mainly by parents with working-class occupations. And again, while any rank order of schools' popularity is unlikely simply to reflect GM or LEA status, our data certainly do not indicate that opting out is likely to lead to diversity based on parity of esteem. Although our sample is only small, our findings suggest that GM status consolidates existing patterns of choice and may well, therefore, contribute to a polarisation of 'desirability' rather than a more level differentiation of local provision.

Opting Out and Increasing Parental Participation

As mentioned in the introduction, a key feature of the GM schools policy is the belief that the 'freeing' of schools from the presumed strictures of LEA control will help them to become better managed and more directly responsive to the needs of parents. Relatedly, opting out is often presented as a means by which parents can escape the policies of some Labour-controlled LEAs where, it is alleged, 'many...feel that their children are trapped in schools...[which] are being used for the promotion of secular and socialist values' (Centre for Policy Studies 1988, p.105). It is seen as providing an opportunity to 'take education out of the hands of planners and return it to parents where it belongs' (ibid. p.108) who 'will enjoy enhanced influence over their conduct' (Rumbold 1989). This is an important argument, for it can be used to combat the criticism that geographical constraints and the friction of distance inevitably impede and undermine parental choice (Ball 1990). From this perspective, GM schools offer parents the opportunity to influence the future of their schools over time, and thus to create choices not previously available. However, as with issues relating to the expansion of choice through new alternatives, we have little evidence to suggest that GM status necessarily implies greater parental control or participation in schools, nor any change of experience for those who attend them.

We do not wish to suggest that those who use GM schools are unsatisfied with them. There is little doubt that the parents and pupils whom we interviewed spoke favourably of their GM experience—nearly all our sample of GM pupils considered their school to be the 'best' in the area. However, such appreciation was not unique to GM schools. Pupils and parents from the LEA and independent sector were equally pleased with the schools which they, or their children, attended. In addition, comparison of levels of parents' expressed

Table 2.3   Parents' reported involvement across sectors

	Involved	*Quite involved*	*Not involved*
GM parents (N = 106)	31%	13%	56%
LEA parents (N = 56)	36%	18%	46%

satisfaction before and after their child's school opted out reveal minimal change.

Just as there is little difference in expressed satisfaction with a school, either since it opted out or between different kinds of school, neither is there any evidence to indicate that GM parents experience greater participation in the governance or general life of their school (cf. Bush et al. 1993). To be sure, parents take part in the voting process if they have children at the school at the time of opting out. Most of the GM parents we interviewed had participated in the ballot, with a large majority voting in favour of GM status. Yet we gained little impression that their support for opting out was based on any desire to participate more fully in the future direction of the school. Indeed, for many parents their backing was more a reflection of loyalty to the headteacher, rather than the result of deliberation on issues surrounding opting out. In schools where the headteacher was heavily involved in promoting GM status, our data would support Roger's (1992) argument that parents often constitute little more than 'ballot-fodder'. Certainly only very few felt that their involvement in the ballot process had given them a greater sense of ownership of the school. And even here, it is hard to see how such a sense of ownership will extend into their child's career, and, perhaps more crucially, through into the next generations of parents.

Similarly, reported levels of parental involvement vary little with school type. In fact, more parents from LEA schools claimed to be involved with their child's schools than those using GM schools (see Table 2.3). Neither are there any significant changes in the reported level of involvement subsequent to opting out. The nature of parental involvement was also constant across sectors. Beyond specific issues relating to their children's progress, parents' involvement in the school centred largely around fund-raising activities. Parents at GM schools were as unlikely as their LEA and independent counterparts to seek involvement in more general issues of school policy, curriculum and pedagogy.

Again, in terms of school governors, there appears to be little clear correlation between school type and familiarity with the governing body. For while 44 per cent of parents with pre-GM entrants claimed they knew at least one of the governors' names, only 26 per cent of post-GM parents did. The greater proportion of pre-GM familiarity might be explained in terms of the high profile of governors in the opt-out ballot. However, the overall level of 'governor' awareness amongst our 'GM' parents (35 per cent) was actually lower than that of their LEA counterparts, where 41 per cent of parents said they were familiar with one or more governors, either in person or by name.

In summary, then, our data do not indicate that GM status, by itself, is having any significant impact on expanding choice, diversifying local provision or increasing parental participation.

The GM Schools Policy in Context

The reasons why any policy fails to fulfil its objectives are, of course, complex and largely conjectural. While Bowe et al. (1992) are surely right to argue that the conventional separation of policy-making from implementation ignores the extent to which policy is recontextualised and recreated in different settings, it is helpful, for analytical purposes, to disentangle features of a particular policy from the context in which it is 'set in motion'. Thus, it seems appropriate to ask if there are aspects of the GM schools policy itself which make it unlikely that opting out will widen opportunity and empower parents through diversifying provision and enhancing parental participation. Or does the policy's limited impact stem from the context in which it is implemented?

There are certainly some who would argue that the GM schools policy will have little effect because it does not go far enough (e.g., Flew 1991). Comparisons from abroad where schools are similarly self-maintained yet 'independent' reveal the limited nature of the 'freedoms' embodied within the GM schools policy. In the rest of Europe, there is a wide diversity of 'independent' schools (Mason 1992). In Denmark, for instance, any group of interested persons can apply for funding to establish their own school, subject only to suitable premises, the appointment of a principal and the guarantee of a small number of pupils in the first two years of operation. Funding is not tied to political orientations, enabling a wide variety of self-governing schools to develop, from those based on particular progressive educational philosophies (e.g., Montessori and Steiner) or political principles (e.g., Marxist) to those catering for particular ethnic and religious groups (e.g., confessional and Muslim schools). In the USA, too, a number of state and county-based reforms (see Chubb and Moe 1990) have been initiated with the intention of devolving control to schools and encouraging self-governance. In 1992, US federal legislation made provisions for the establishment of 'charter schools'. Like GM schools, these schools will operate outside local district control. But, unlike current GM schools, they will be 'new' in a far more fundamental sense in that they can be started by any group which can demonstrate sufficient commitment (Wohlstetter and Anderson 1992).

Such comparisons make it clear that, despite the British government's rhetoric of 'freedom' and 'self-determination', the provisions embodied within the GM schools policy offer as many constraints as possibilities. Although the policy enables schools to 'break free of the local authority', it is an exaggeration to claim that this means these schools have been given 'full control of their own destinies' (Conservative Party 1992).

In the first place, all operating GM schools are existing institutions. They are not only already established, but had to be 'viable' in terms of pupil recruitment in order to obtain the Secretary of State's approval for GM status. Such schools are therefore under little pressure from 'market forces' to alter already 'successful' reputations and practices.

Second, GM schools are obliged to teach the National Curriculum alongside their LEA counterparts. It is hard to see how they are able to devise curricula which might prove more attractive to parents than the present arrangements. The relationship between the compulsory introduction of a fairly tightly specified curriculum and the devolution of power from 'monopoly' providers to consumers is, of course, not straightforward. Although Whitty (1989) suggests the articulation of the National Curriculum with other elements of ERA might be less contradictory than some commentators have suggested, full blooded advocates of the education 'market' are less convinced. As Flew (1991) argues, the potential of 'demonopolization' through opting out and LMS 'has to a considerable extent been neutralized and frustrated by the intrusions of the dominant directive and centralizing drive towards a more intensive and uniform monopolistic provision' (p.43).

Third, each one of our sample of GM schools was obliged to

preserve their 'character' on incorporation. Indeed, this was a precondition of them 'going GM'. Schools may apply for a subsequent change of character, but such changes must be argued for and are subject to the Secretary of State's approval. It is useful at this point to contrast the GM schools policy with another government strategy aimed at diversifying educational provision, namely, the CTC initiative. If, as Edwards et al. (1992a) argue, CTCs are 'obliged to be different', GM schools, it appears, were initially obliged to be the 'same'. And, although some would claim that protecting existing alternatives, especially grammar schools, is an important dimension of choice, it does not constitute an *expansion* of choice. So far, then, it is only possible to argue that GM status represents preservation rather than innovation.

Correspondingly, in terms of enhancing 'consumer power' through increased parental participation, the GM schools policy provides no clearer lines of communication and accountability than other state-maintained schools. Certainly, parents with children at the school are able to petition for GM status and participate in any subsequent ballot. Indeed, parent representatives are now compelled to consider opting out in their capacity as school governors. But once a school has opted out, the nature and degree of parental and community influence through the governing body is highly ambiguous. The case of Stratford School, Newham (1992), where the head and her chair of governors came into direct conflict, necessitating central government intervention (Anon 1992), provides an illustration of the ways in which parental/community control, which is perceived as 'inappropriate', can be overridden.

It might appear, then, as if the statutory and interventionist controls outlined above constrain the ability of GM schools to diversify provision and enhance parental control. If this is the case, then the policies outlined within the 1992 Education White Paper and 1993 Education Act might offer greater promise. Although future GM schools will still be obliged to follow the National Curriculum, they are actively encouraged to diversify through specialisation. Schools are now able to select a minority of pupils on the basis of ability and aptitude. Although selection on general academic ability is certainly a key feature of the new proposals, it is not the only 'specialisation' which is being encouraged. Along with the now familiar drive for promoting technology and the aim to establish 'technology colleges' to supplement existing technology schools and CTCs, schools are invited to emphasise other curricular specialisations, for instance, through selecting pupils with particular aptitudes in languages, music or sport. In addition, mechanisms are to be put in place which allow a school opting out to apply simultaneously for a change in size or character. There are also procedures to allow the creation of new GM schools by voluntary agreement.

Our research, on the other hand, gives us few grounds for believing that these new measures will contribute to diversity of school provision and greater empowerment of parents. The reasons for this, however, are not merely to do with the regulated autonomy which GM schools 'enjoy'; they relate too to the context within which the policy has been implemented.

In terms of parental participation, for instance, there is nothing legally to prevent parents from being more directive in their children's education. We have argued earlier in this paper that, in many cases, parents appear little more than 'ballot-fodder' in the vote on opting out. We have also suggested elsewhere (Halpin et al. 1994) that GM status is more of a headteachers' than a parents' charter. But this stems not so much from the policy, as from the power of the teaching profession.

Parental 'empowerment' can extend further than simply selecting a school. It might be exercised in many other areas, such as the curriculum, teaching activities and teachers themselves (Raywid 1985). Such options, though, are rarely even thought of, let alone made available. There is, as Ashworth et al. (1988) point out, 'no technical reason why choice should not be exercised in these areas but they do not seem to be part of the debate' (p.13). To some extent the limits on the debate are set within the current policy discourse. It is quite clear that government strategies to 'empower' parents concentrate on what Hirschmann (1970) refers to as 'exit' rather than 'voice'. In addition, the government's notion of 'empowerment' is fairly unfocused and sloganistic. The concept is, therefore, 'meaningless, beyond a superficial level, merely offering a symbolic gloss of popular democracy, and freedom from (usually local) state bureaucracy' (Vincent 1993a).

However, the framing of New Right discourse is not the only limit on more radical notions of what parental empowerment might embody. The teaching profession is equally resistant. Although their 'professional autonomy' has no doubt been threatened and, in some areas, diminished, by the central state, there is little to suggest that recent policies have resulted in a reformulation of teacher—parent relations. Even in environments designed to enhance parental involvement, the authority vested in professional interests is used to devalue, marginalise and, in many cases, channel lay participation into non-controversial areas, such as fund-raising activities. Vincent (1993b), for instance, illustrates how various initiatives in community participation tend to preserve rather than alter existing power relations. Parents' involvement is limited to concerns over how they can help their individual child, rather than matters of school policy. Research on the role of parents on governing bodies reveals similar patterns, where professional authority derived from specialist knowledge overrides effective lay participation (Deem et al. 1991). Parent governors, in particular, tend to be the least participative (Brehony 1992, Golby and Brigley 1989), again 'supporting' professionals in their tasks rather than monitoring or contesting them. In GM schools, the asymmetry of power between lay participants and professionals is still apparent in models of 'good practice' where discussion centres on 'managing and educating the governing body' (Deem and Wilkins 1992, p.76).

Even where parental voices are effective, it is more than likely they will be not just those that are the loudest and most persistent, but those which speak the same language as the professionals. Brehony (1992) comments on how women, working-class and black governors tend to be less active in governors' meetings where they are 'at best ignored and at worst interrupted' (p.210). These processes of marginalisation stem as much from 'professional' definitions of 'appropriate' cultural resources as from the limits of policy. There is therefore little reason to suppose that those whose voices have, in the past, either been silent, or ignored, will benefit in the near future.

The apparent 'failure' of GM schools to diversify local provision is similarly difficult to account for in terms of the policy alone. Although the National Curriculum is undoubtedly prescriptive, it is not necessarily the strait-jacket which it is often made out to be. As Bowe et al. (1992) argue, the interpretation and adaptation of policy is not only possible, but inevitable. Their own research, for example, reveals that the National Curriculum 'is not so much being "implemented" in schools as being "recreated", not so much "reproduced" as "produced"' (p.120). There is nothing to prevent schools innovating and specialising, albeit within limits. Money to enable GM schools to develop their technology curriculum is readily available from the Technology in Schools Initiative. Indeed, some of our sample of GM schools have received funding from this source. Not one of them, however, was willing to emphasise this or market their schools along technological lines.

The reinvigorated traditionalism of our sample of GM schools alluded to earlier, and also evident in some of the LEA schools as well, may well be leading to the dull uniformity of which Stephen Ball speaks (this volume). But, again, this does not stem from the policy, or indeed, the government's expressed intentions. Although some might say such schools are following the government's implicit perception of 'good practice', there is nothing within the terms of the legislation to prevent them from modelling themselves along alternative lines.

The CTC initiative provides a clear illustration of the extent to which forms of specialisation are resisted. Despite their favourable funding, the early experience of CTCs suggests that, far from 'breaking the mould', they offer little that is radically different from other schools and have yet to shift away from traditional modes of 'academic' teaching and learning (Walford and Miller 1991, Edwards et al. 1992b).

The lack of curricular specialisation and diversification of provision has to be viewed within the British context where 'educational innovation has persistently failed when it has diverged too sharply from the academic model firmly entrenched in the high status private sector and in the more favoured public schools' (Edwards and Whitty 1993, p.113). That 'equal but different' alternatives to traditional modes of schooling are unlikely to develop can be seen in the low profile of GM technology schools. Recent DFE progress reports reveal that only seven of the 554 secondary schools which have opted out incorporate the terms 'technical' or 'technology' within their name. Furthermore, it is worth noting that five of these seven 'specialist' schools are located in areas which still operate a strong selective system. Such 'niche-marketing' is therefore as much a response to firmly entrenched hierarchies as a challenge to them. Indeed, in contexts where 'diversification' operates to compensate for formally stratified provision, it is likely to endorse, rather than diminish, the perceived 'superiority' of the academic model.

That measures to diversify provision are likely to flounder resides in the fact that each school's educational identity is forged through its relationship to other elements in the system. Unlike many other 'commodities', education is not an 'absolute', but a 'positional' good (Hirsch 1977, Miliband 1992), the value of which is determined by its scarcity. The attractiveness or desirability of one particular school and the kind of 'goods' it offers is not dependent on its *actual* qualities, but on its *relative* position to other forms of provision. Hierarchical relations between schools are, therefore, to some extent inevitable consequences of the linkage between education and a stratified socio-economic structure. It is hard to see how any education policy alone is capable of addressing this relationship.

Such an argument raises particular difficulties for the formulation of alternative education policies. For it implies than no policy, whether it emanates from the Left or Right, will be successful in enhancing educational opportunities within the existing context.

This does not necessarily mean a retreat into pessimism, however. If we believe that wider opportunities and greater democratisation of education are important objectives, it might be worth considering ways in which the failure of opting out and other educational reforms can inform future policies.

It might, for example, be important to move the debate beyond issues of access and exit. Of course, choice of school is important. Indeed, as discussed earlier, within recent policies it constitutes the principal form of accountability. On the other hand, while agreeing with Ball et al. (1993) that such policies exacerbate the inequalities which various consumers bring to the market place, education has long been an area in which it was important for parents to take and preserve the leading edge. The middle classes have always been able to manipulate and colonise educational opportunities, be it the tripartite system (e.g., Jackson and Marsden 1967), comprehensivisation (Ford 1969), or even specifically targeted policies such as the Assisted Places Scheme (Edwards et al. 1989). It is hard to envisage a policy initiative directed at access alone which will be resistant to such forces.

Maybe, then, we should move our attention away from access as the principal determinant of opportunity and focus on what goes on *inside* the school, that is, on the quality of provision, as measured along a number of criteria, and the mechanisms of local account-ability. Anticipating specific policies is by no means easy, but it may require us to explore alternative forms of educational governance that encourage moves towards a more participatory democracy 'in which the ways and means of involving people much more closely in the process of self-government can be learned and extended' (Williams 1961: 343).

3 THE POLITICAL ECONOMY OF LOCAL MANAGEMENT OF SCHOOLS[1]

Hywel Thomas and Alison Bullock

Five components of the 1988 Education Reform Act together create a market-like system in which schools can be expected to compete against each other in attempts to attract pupils. These are: a scheme of *financial delegation* whereby schools are given day-to-day control over their budget and are required to live within this cash-limited allocation; a new system of *formula funding* in which most of the money delegated is based upon the number of pupils on roll; changes in *admissions regulations* which require schools to admit pupils to the physical capacity of the building; a form of *staffing delegation* which make schools responsible for the appointment and dismissal of staff; and more emphasis upon *performance indicators* intended to provide parents with information about the schools in this 'market'. That the jobs of teachers depend upon pupil numbers in a system where the exercise of parental preferences as between schools is encouraged can be expected to make this *pupil-as-voucher* system—more formally known as Local Management of Schools (LMS)—one of the more potent changes of the 1988 Act.

The market-like nature of LMS contributes to its potency and the associated concerns, because markets have foreseeable consequences which, even if unintended, can mean injustice for the least well resourced in our society. Pressures on schools to compete may cause them to seek some pupils more than others and, in a system where examination results are published annually, there may be a temptation to attract those who can be relied upon to do well. We fully recognise that such dangers are associated with markets and share the concern of others that the privileging consequences of markets are not only undesirable but require resistance. Such resistance and the development of alternative policies requires an initial analysis of the political economy in which schools function. We argue that the political economy of schools is not reducible to a choice between market and

41

non-market alternatives and it is with this theme that the paper begins. This will be followed by a section which draws upon a recently completed research project to illustrate some of the diversity in the systems which are emerging and concludes with some comments on its implications.

Education as a Mixed Economy[2]

Accounts about the emergence of markets in education appear often to overlook their presence before 1988. The housing market has long had an effect upon the nature of intakes to schools. The labour market allows teachers to choose the schools in which they wish to teach. It may be that the housing and labour markets are so familiar to us that they have almost become invisible. If such is the case, might we also overlook the net benefits these markets bring?

We do not need to become blind adherents to market forms in order to recognise that they have some appeal, more especially when viewed against likely alternatives. How many teachers in Britain, for example, would express a preference for a system of employment where, at the end of their training period, they were directed to teach in a specific school 'somewhere in Britain'? What enthusiasm would there be for a system which abolished the market in book publishing and produced the only texts which were to be used in teaching? How extensive would be the support for a housing policy which directed where we lived as a means of ensuring that the neighbourhood of each school contained a distribution of social groups which reflected the national pattern? Certain equity benefits attach to each of these three options but they compete with other compelling human rights. We might also recognise that, as with market forms, command systems have unwelcome characteristics, including scope for corruption as officials dispense favours.

Faced with a choice between market forms and systems of command and control, then, the choice is by no means straightforward. It is, however, a false prospectus. We are not required to choose between market systems and command systems. Rather, we are faced with complex mixed economies which bear some market characteristics but also have some element of command—and more. Alongside markets and command, we need to take account of those circumstances where resources are allocated on the basis of other factors.

The self-image and rhetoric of professional groups, for example, often lay claim to modes of behaviour which place the interests of clients ahead of those of the service provider. We do not need to accept such a rhetoric uncritically and we must also recognise the self-interest which underlies paid employment (teaching is not a vocation!) but we should not also dismiss the readiness of some to work long hours in demanding environments because of moral codes which include principles of service to others.

Markets, command and professionalism, then, co-exist within a mixed economy of schools. Whilst the contemporary mixed economy has some very evident market-like features, what is also clear is that these market-like features are regulated through command systems. These command systems can play a key role in regulating the market-like features so that the privileging associated with conventional markets may work in favour of the least well-resourced. In addition, the behaviour of professional groups may not be explicable in market terms and their decisions may confound the outcomes expected from conventional markets.

In summary, local management has reworked the mixed economy within which schools function. What has to be analysed is not the emergence of markets but the nature of these restructured mixed economies. How the rules for funding schools play a role in these mixed economies has been examined more fully elsewhere. In this paper, we draw only upon some work on the funding of additional educational needs.

Funding Additional Educational Needs

The national guidelines for funding schools have allowed LEAs considerable latitude in regulating the funding of pupils with additional educational needs. When we examine formula allocations to individual schools, we find that funds for additional educational needs can account for nothing or, at the other extreme, more than 20 per cent of a school's formula budget before any transitional adjustments. Table 3.1 presents information on the additional educational needs (AEN) funding, adding together allocations from both social and special educational factors, as a percentage of each school's formula budget.

From the 1990/91 data from almost 2800 primary and secondary schools in thirteen LEAs, it can be seen that 17 per cent of schools are

Table 3.1 Additional Educational Needs Allocations as Percentages of Formula Budgets

AEN as % Formula	n schools	valid percent
0	468	17
more than 0 to 1%	637	23
<1 to 2%	396	14
<2 to 3%	212	8
<3 top 4%	185	7
<4 to 5%	197	7
<5 to 6%	153	5.5
<6 to 7%	77	3
<7 to 8%	82	3
<8 to 9%	73	3
<9 to 10%	50	2
<10 to 15%	163	6
<15 to 20%	57	2
more than 20%	42	1.5
Total	2792	

not eligible for additional educational needs (AEN) funding. For a further 37 per cent of schools, sums allocated for AEN are greater than zero and up to 2 per cent of their formula budgets. AEN funding is between 2 per cent and 5 per cent for 21 per cent of schools; 5 per cent to 10 per cent for more than 16 per cent of these schools, and more than 10 per cent of their formula budget for over 9 per cent of the schools. When the information is considered for each LEA in our data set, considerable variation is found (Bullock and Thomas 1994).

In our main report, we proceed to provide a more detailed analysis of the AEN provision in each of our thirteen LEAs. Following such descriptions, we explored whether and how the change to formula funding has affected the level of funding of schools serving pupils with additional educational needs. We compare each school's historic budget[3] with its formula budget, dividing schools into two groups: 'winning' schools, in the sense that a school's formula budget is more than its historic budget, and 'losing' school in the sense that the formula budget is less than the historic budget. The size of the loss or gain has also been calculated, as a percentage of formula budget. We then ask whether there is any relationship between the size of the loss or gain and the size of the AEN allocation. Is it the case, for instance, that schools with comparatively large AEN allocations are more highly represented in the 'losing' group? Or is it the case that, as the percentage of formula allocated on the basis of AEN increases, so the size of the loss decreases?[4]

For ten of our thirteen LEAs we were able to explore such hypotheses and they are reported. In this chapter we illustrate that data with three cases.

County A

This county has one AEN factor which distributes 5.1 per cent of the total budget share, funds being allocated on the basis of Free School Meals (FSMs) take-up. Within the scheme, the allocation of funds is described as follows:

> Depending on the proportion of pupils in receipt of a free school meal, the pupil numbers in the school are weighted by a factor (see below). The weighted pupil numbers for each school are expressed as a proportion of the total for all schools and this proportion is applied to the amount of the ASB allocated by this factor.

The percentage of FSMs take-up is banded and weighted as follows:

Primary

% take-up of FSM	0 to 4%	4 to 8.5%	8.5 to 13%	13 to 20%	20%+
pupils weighted by	0	0.5	1.0	1.5	2.0

Secondary

% take-up of FSM	0 to 2%	2 to 5.5%	5.5 to 9%	9 to 12%	12%+
pupils weighted by	0	0.75	1.0	2.0	2.5

Thus, in the primary sector, schools with 4 per cent or fewer pupils in receipt of FSMs will not be eligible for additional AEN funding. This eligibility percentage is 2 per cent in the secondary sector. A school's socio-economic needs allocation is allocated as the number on roll multiplied by the appropriate weighting, multiplied by the cash amount. In the year 1990/91 this amount was £89.

In exploring whether the change to formula funding has affected the level of funding of schools serving pupils with additional educational needs, we correlated the size of loss/gain with the percentage of formula on social needs. This gave a correlation value of 0.49**.[5] The positive association suggests that the more (proportionally) a school receives for AEN, the greater the size of the gain. In other words, schools which are high on the AEN factor are more likely to be 'winners' in the transition to formula funding. When primary and secondary sectors are considered separately, a stronger positive association is found in the primary sector.[6]

In short, whether intentionally or not, the change to formula funding has tended to favour schools serving AEN pupils.

Borough B

This borough's formula includes a special needs related factor that is based on the proportion of pupils from socially disadvantaged backgrounds and accounts for 3.2 per cent of the LEA's total budget share. For the year 1990/91, primary schools were banded, 'placement being related to criteria reflecting the socio-economic composition of the school's catchment area'. The additional allocations for each band were equivalent to increases in the element for teachers' salaries. Primary schools in Bands 1 and 2 received no additions; Band 3 schools gained 3.3 per cent; Band 4, 10 per cent and Band 5 schools 16.6 per cent. In the secondary sector also, schools received additional funding related to the socio-economic composition of the catchment area, although these schools were not actually banded. Examples of allocations in the primary sector include £5,599 for a Band 3 primary school with 314 pupils on roll; £23,349 for a Band 5 school with 226 pupils. All schools in the secondary sector received in excess of £50,000 for special needs and two received over £100,000.

The results of the statistical correlations between size of loss/gain and the level of special needs related funding are given below:

All schools	*Primary*	*Secondary*
– 0.44**	– 0.31**	– 0.72**

The association between the two variables is negative. It is strongest in the secondary sector, suggesting that secondary schools in catchment areas with high levels of pupils from socially disadvantaged areas tend to be the more sizeable losers: in other words, the size of the gain diminishes as the proportion of AEN funding increases. However, if the three biggest losers are excluded, a non-significant correlation value of -0.15 is given. The negative association is weak in the primary sector and reduced to -0.26** with the exclusion of the biggest loser. The weak to moderate negative association produced when the borough is considered as a whole reduces to -0.30** if the four biggest losers are excluded.

Borough C

Borough C's AEN factor comprises a social needs element (based on entitlement to FSMs and amounting to 7 per cent of the LEA's budget share) and funding for special needs (using numbers of statemented pupils and amounting to 0.5 per cent of the total budget share). Social needs funding is calculated as £557.44 × FSMs numbers. For special needs, each statemented pupil receives an additional £1,162.

Shown below are the correlation values for the AEN variables and the size of loss/gain variable. Funding for statemented pupils, the special needs factor, was not found to be associated with size of loss/gain: none of the correlation values, for all schools or schools by sector, were statistically significant (any association may have been due to chance). However a low positive correlation (r = 0.26*) was produced for the whole set of schools when the four schools with the highest level of special needs funding were excluded. The positive value suggests that size of gain increases (or loss decreases) as level of special needs funding increases. The association, however, is low.

	All schools	Primary	Secondary
All social needs	0.67**	0.65**	0.46
special needs	- 0.17	- 0.17	- 0.51
both AEN factors	0.64**	0.63**	0.30

In the primary sector alone, however, a strong association was found to exist between level of social needs funding and size of loss/gain. In the secondary sector, on the other hand, there was no significant association. The positive direction of the primary correlation value suggests that as the proportion of the allocation based on social needs increases so the size gain increases. Put another way, generally, the less money (proportionally) a school receives for FSMs pupils, the greater the size of loss. Similar correlation values are produced when the two AEN factors are combined.

In brief then, although correlations tell us nothing about causal relationships between variables, there are some indications that Borough C may have devised a formula that favours primary schools serving pupils with additional educational needs.

Since Borough C has two AEN factors, we explored the association between them: would there be indications that schools serving pupils with social needs were a similar set of schools with statemented pupils? The correlation figures[7] show no association between the AEN factors, in the first instance, although, after excluding outliers, a weak correlation ($r = 0.28^{**}$) is given for all schools. In the primary sector the exclusion of outliers produces a correlation value of 0.24^*. Such correlations suggest an association between the two AEN factors, such that schools eligible for social needs funding tend to be similar to the set of schools serving statemented pupils. The correlations are, however, weak. In the secondary sector the exclusion of outliers did not result in a statistically signicant correlation coefficient.

Additional Needs and the Political Economy of LMS

Although in many ways the DFE and Welsh Office framework for local management is prescriptive and restrictive, evidence from our set of LEAs shows the scope for diversity in local policies. For schools serving pupils with additional educational needs, the analysis shows substantial differences in the nature of local management schemes. It appears from our analysis that the national framework for local management has been sufficiently flexible to allow some LEAs to direct resources in such a way that the greatest beneficiaries have been schools with the highest proportion of pupils with additional educational needs. Far from being a regressive change, in these LEAs LMS has led to an apparent initial redistribution of resources benefiting the least advantaged. Equally, in other LEAs the effect of LMS has been in the opposite direction, those schools with a high proportion of pupils with additional educational needs being the losers in the change of funding. Without further study, including interviews with key participants in the design of a formula, we cannot provide an account of how these outcomes occurred. What is evident, however, is that the initial *change* to LMS has not had a simple one-way effect leading to greater disadvantage for pupils with additional educational needs; in some LEAs schools with high levels of pupils with AEN have been net beneficiaries of the changes in funding.

We are, of course, unable to predict *future* patterns of competition and levels of resourcing from these data. If the environment becomes increasingly competitive it may be that schools will wish to avoid pupils with additional educational needs because of concern that they will not perform well in examination league tables. The future may, however, be more complex. Our data show some LEAs providing substantial additional resources. To the extent that schools will wholly absorb an ethos of self-interest, therefore, high levels of AEN funding may shape their preferences and influence their 'marketing' strategies. It may be the case, for example, that high levels of support for pupils with additional educational needs will cause schools already serving those communities to be less likely to 'market' themselves to new client groups. If schools are on the boundary of communities with high levels of social deprivation, might they be less concerned with their recruitment patterns if there were no differential in funding?

These questions assume a dominance of self-interested behaviour but are we right to do so? Writing recently on the contemporary appeal to greater self-interest, Ware (1990) asks: 'does market society corrode altruism?' (p.185). It is a natural antithesis of Titmuss's (1970) view that social policy reforms such as the creation of the National Health Service served to recognise and encourage altruistic behaviour. Our data at least raise the possibility that the outcomes of LMS may differ between LEAs, at least in some part because of the configuration of the local funding formula. Are the decision-makers in schools minded to behave differently—less competitively—in an LEA where the formula lays more emphasis on resourcing additional educational needs as compared with an LEA which does not?

Our tentative—and wholly speculative—answer would be: probably not if that alone distinguished one LEA's policy context from another! That is not to say that the focus of competitive behaviour would not be affected. The more important question would be to consider what other regulatory devices may interact with the formula to create the conditions which appeal more to wider conceptions of altruism and the needs of less privileged pupils.

Restructuring the Political Economy of LMS

It is likely that many features of LMS will survive any foreseeable change of government. Delegation, transparent formula-based funding and more information for parents are also, in principle, welcome innovations. It is also to be hoped that we do not return to the spurious 'efficiency' arguments of the 1980 Education Act for holding admissions to schools below capacity. Approval and support of these principles, however, does not mean support for their present application and the scarcely veiled preferences of government ministers for greater differentation or their apparent lack of concern about any consequent inequality. We examine alternatives briefly by reviewing options for a more progressive mixed economy for funding, admissions and performance information.

Formula funding rules can always be rewritten to lay down minimum rules about the allocation of funds to schools with high levels of pupils with additional educational needs. We suggest that such an explicit approach to funding is to be preferred to the old system which relied upon various combinations of custom, practice, political and/or officer discretion and sheer ignorance.

Changes in rules governing admissions are central to the creation of a 'market', and the pressures upon headteachers to ensure institutional survival places a premium on their presenting their school in ways which will appeal to parents and pupils. The specific form of regulations governing admissions is, therefore, a crucial area in its consequence for competition. Regulations must be determined at the level of the local school system and clearly specified so that decision-making is not captured by individual schools. The more complex the criteria, for example, the greater the scope for school-based interpretation and choice. How funding and admissions interact with staff tenure is another key component of the political economy. The authors of this chapter differ in what they believe to be an appropriate strategy. Whilst one (Hywel Thomas) would accept a form of managed competition with jobs dependent upon recruitment, the other (Alison Bullock) has concerns about the implications of such a position and would wish to return to a position close to that established by the 1986 Education Act.[8]

Where we agree is that there is a debate needed as to whether citizens' rights in relation to school choice can best be secured by means of empowerment through managed competition or democratic accountability (see Plant, 1990, p.21 for a brief discussion). In any event, we believe that system management should go wider than regulating admissions rules. This can include LEAs deciding to weight funding formulae to the advantage of pupils for whom English is a second language or who have non-statemented special needs, and/or pupils from socially disadvantaged backgrounds. It can also include LEAs providing value-added data on school performance.

The information reported about schools can be increased in scope, partly by surveying parents and pupils on a range of factors and then publishing their assessment of provision. Recent material on school ethos indicators prepared for the Scottish Office provides interesting examples of what is possible here (Scottish Office 1992a; 1992b). Its importance is that it makes schools more likely to address a wider range of performance areas and thereby include a more educative concept of parental choice—as continuing dialogue—than the entry/ exit choices of the conventional market.

Conclusion: LEAs and LMS

It has been the purpose of this chapter to argue that there is no simple choice between markets and hierarchies as a basis for deciding how educational goods and services shall be produced; but rather, that it is a condition of a pluralist society that these different mechanisms of resource allocation co-exist, appealing to different aspects of human motive, and resolving them with a variety of emphasis between the individual and the collective. What is required is the resolution of the complex balance(s) to be struck between the variety of means by which education services are produced and allocated in our society. Policies have to be devised, therefore, which take account of this mixed economy.

We have indicated that within the existing framework of LMS, LEAs have devised distinctive approaches to funding and that these have diverse consequences for pupils. We have also outlined ways in which, within the principles of LMS, rules can be altered to reflect quite different social and educational goals from those of the present government. Our proposals have implications for the local government of education. Managing admissions and managing performance information within a more progressive funding regime provides LEAs with the means by which they can develop a role as the representative of parents and pupils in a form of purchaser-provider relationship. Such a purchaser-provider relationship would differ considerably from the variant creating problems in the health service. In a system where schools remain significant centres of delegated management, LEAs can act as agents collecting and reporting on the performance of schools, offering schools, parents and pupils information on school processes and performance. By maintaining a managed admissions system with rules set by the LEA, whilst allowing schools to admit to their capacity, it can provide space for pupil and parental preferences. The resulting mixed economy would still allow pupil and parental preferences to shape the system but in ways which limit the nature of competition.

A revised political economy for LMS means reserving to the centre (central and local government) mechanisms of resource allocation—funding levels and rules, admission arrangements, some performance information and some performance reporting—whilst allowing localities (parents, pupils, school staff, governing bodies) to resolve the means for making decisions within that framework (more discretion over the curriculum, staffing and other resource decisions).

PART 2
CURRICULUM AND TEACHERS

4 AN ALTERNATIVE NATIONAL CURRICULUM

Philip O'Hear

As we have the final report by Sir Ron Dearing (Dearing 1994) of his review of the National Curriculum and its Assessment, rapidly and completely accepted by the Conservative government, it may appear odd to continue to argue for an alternative national curriculum. This may seem even more unnecessary when the scale and scope of the changes proposed by Dearing, and the evident extent to which he has sought to find and build on a professional consensus, are considered. In this chapter, I will argue that, despite Dearing's considerable achievement in grasping some central political and educational issues and developing clear and considered proposals for rationalisation and simplification, the 1994 national curriculum remains deeply flawed. The need for a coherent alternative, therefore, continues to be strong.

Starting from adequately developed aims about education and its place in our society, there is not only a strong case for a National Curriculum but a coherent direction for developing it. Sadly, Dearing has not returned far enough to first principles in his major reform of the 1988 structure and the overbearing assessment model imposed upon it by a government concerned with regulating teachers in whom it seemed to have no trust. By 1993 we faced a set of issues that caused major problems in our planning, such as what to prescribe and what to guide, the role for subjects and topic work, the extent and place for student choice and the shape and nature of the assessment instruments. There was almost universal agreement among educationalists, teachers, parents and governors, despite many serious differences about aspects of content and purpose of the curriculum, that the current assessment procedures had the potential to do enormous damage. This consensus provided a context for the teacher union boycotts of the statutory tests that led to a reversal of much of government policy. The formation of the Schools Curriculum and Assessment Authority, and the appointment of Dearing to lead its work by seeking the views of professionals and parents and with the power to make wholesale and rapid change were concrete and welcome results of new thinking and direction in policy. Because, however, the brief for Dearing's work arose so directly from a concern to deal with the wreckage of a flagship policy (simple pencil and paper tests with league tables of results at all ages) in the face of a rare industrial relations defeat, the consequent reform has been political rather than educational.

One significant factor in the direction of the Dearing reforms has been the nature of the justification used by the teacher unions to win the right to the boycott of the 1993 tests when challenged in the courts. To fall within the scope of legitimate industrial action, the boycott had to be presented on grounds of resistance to imposed and unfair workload. This, rather than educational arguments against the nature of the tests that had been developed, or the way these tests were giving weight to skill and content aspects of subjects, came to dominate the public and, even, the professional debate. Dearing's brief to simplify the curriculum, make its testing and record keeping less onerous, reduce subjects to their core and to review the ten level all age linear scale of progress was conceived and, largely, carried out as though all these were largely pragmatic tasks that would take their own rational shape if adequate consultation and enough good sense were applied in the process.

In our paper 'A National Curriculum For All: Laying the Foundations for Success' (O'Hear and White 1991), John White and I argued for a fundamental review of the 1988 National Curriculum. The outcome should have been a broader but less prescriptive curriculum based on overall aims, rather than the differently con-ceived content of 10 subjects, themselves chosen arbitrarily. In our model, recognition of teachers' professionalism and knowledge of the learning needs and potential of their pupils would be given by allowing them a good deal of control of the content, order and delivery of the curriculum. We argued for an assessment structure that would value the teacher's understanding of the pupil's progress and be focused on supporting progress and partnership between pupil, family and school and we made a strong case for a significant degree of pupil choice in what and when to learn, particularly at age 14 and beyond. Dearing's concerns for valuing the work of teachers in planning and assessing work, his intention to reduce workload and to allow for flexibility and some pupil choice are all welcome and go a long way towards some of the specific proposals we set out in 1991. They do not, however, set the planning of the curriculum in a context of clearly established aims, nor do they extend our notion of content beyond the ten subjects, and they still present a confused, potentially damaging, approach to assessment.

I will now outline the structure we proposed that does, by contrast, offer a coherent approach to the whole of the curriculum and its assessment. As I do so, I will develop my criticisms of the Dearing reforms in the areas just mentioned. I will start, however, further back from these specifics than Dearing's brief encouraged him to do. We must start our approach with a notion of 'real education' that considers the whole child as a future citizen and which plans what should be learned in terms of the whole curriculum. This will rescue the concept of real education from those who use it to campaign for simple tests and rote learning. Rather, it leads us to develop practice that integrates assessment with teaching to enhance motivation and progress whilst also ensuring continuity. It will require us to address ways of constructing meaningful links in curriculum areas such as science and technology, the arts as a whole, the humanities and social and personal education.

Such a national curriculum would set planning at a national and school level in the context of coherent and clear aims and values. Central to our society and its well-being is the ideal of liberal democracy. Drawing on this ideal and its prime values of self determination and the recognition of our interdependence on each other, we can articulate the personal qualities needed for a self-determined and socially aware life. These personal qualities are the preconditions of citizenship in a liberal democracy and thus part of the entitlement and obligation of each citizen. These can be classified into three broad areas:

☐ personal concerns
(managing one's own needs, pursuing personal projects, developing qualities of character);

☐ social involvement and concern for others
(working for shared goals, enjoying friends, family, developing more general social responsibility, refraining from harming others, being impartial);

☐ critical and reflective awareness
(self knowledge, including openness, reflection on priorities among one's values, critical awareness and so on).

All these personal qualities have an educational dimension in that their development requires the systematic acquisition of knowledge, understanding, attitudes and competencies. Since possession of them is a fundamental requirement for self-determining and socially responsible participation in a liberal democratic society, it is quite proper that these values should inform our educational planning, both nationally and in schools. Moreover, we can draw up a framework for the curriculum, derived from the personal qualities, that includes the *content* of the curriculum, *the wider curriculum* within the life of an effective school, a *structure for progression and choice*, and the *system for assessment and recording*.

Because this framework is at a higher conceptual level than any of the specific details of the operational curriculum, it provides a focused and coherent set of reference points against which to make the decisions of selection, structure and emphasis involved in operational planning. The lack of such a conceptual framework in the present National Curriculum lays it open to the arbitrary backtrackings and pressure group hijackings that have characterised the first five years of its implementation. The ten subject starting point of the present National Curriculum, rather than providing the clear and universally understandable account of the curriculum required by Parliamentary draft writers, is fundamentally inadequate.

Dearing, however, has strengthened rather than weakened the place of subjects in the whole. The slimming down he proposes is entirely in terms of the ten subjects with the cross-curricular aspects looking increasingly marginalised. The slimming down will be done by small working parties (mostly representing a good cross-section of teacher and educational thinking, but with a powerful role for the right-wing advisers who continue to have the ear of the Government) who will start from the existing Orders and, by and large, consider their subject in isolation. All this fails to recognise that slimming down, just as much as the establishment of contents, is not a neutral process. In the detailed decisions of what aspects of knowledge, understanding and skills are to remain in the compulsory core, major issues of value and teaching methodology will be determined.

The currently proposed changes in English and Technology (which are to be taken as the starting point for the slimming down in these subjects) illustrate this well. In English, a particular view of the way language competences develop in children, and of the relationship of the vernacular language of the child to the acquisition of standard English, has been set into the detailed criteria for planning and assessing the subject. The assessment, as set out in the proposed new statements of attainment, will focus on certain skills in a way that reduces the integration of reading, writing and discussion that HMI, teachers and most educationalists have seen as strengths of the original orders, associated with raised achievement. Similarly, the proposed revisions in Technology place increased weight on fabrication, use of control technology and experience of resistant materials as against open-ended design work, model making and light craft. These proposals have been much welcomed since they remove a good deal of current uncertainty, even vagueness. In both subjects, the original review and slimming down have produced a sharp change of value and emphasis, welcome in the case of Technology (if difficult to resource) and unwelcome in English (if easier to test by external examination).

The slimming down has enormous significance, even though a great deal else will be offered as possible additional material, with which schools will be able to set a fuller, or more holistic, context and approach for the teaching of the statutory core. But there is the rub. It is the new slim core that will be compulsory and, thus, the basis of the assessment and record keeping, an issue to which I shall return later. Without a more satisfactory conceptual base than a simple list of subjects, any curriculum is going to be open to inconsistent change and excessive prescription as different views of learning and national need are fought out in the detail rather than in the original design. This, I suspect, will be the crunch in the debates of the subject groups working on the proposals for slimming down the curriculum. And we still do not know why, precisely, it is these ten subjects that have been chosen, why social studies, drama and dance are excluded, why the focus in history should be so weighted to pre-twentieth-century Britain and so on. The framework developed in our IPPR paper is an attempt to show that it is both possible and helpful to set out an original design for the curriculum in which these crucial issues of detail and selection—which have such a powerful impact on the values transmitted and the style of teaching—can be resolved consistently and coherently. Moreover, a proper framework for evaluating and modifying can also be developed if the core aims are clear and we will need neither the continual upheavals of the first five years of the 1988 National Curriculum nor Dearing's somewhat chilling promise of no further change for five years after his reforms are in place.

In terms of *the content of the curriculum*, we identify the knowledge, understanding, experience of the arts and practical competencies required for possession of the personal qualities. Often the content we describe is familiar, which is hardly surprising since there is very broad consensus about the main elements of compulsory content. Our framework, however, shows the relevance of content to educational and social values and indicates how the selection of content can be based on this relevance and not simply on assertion and whim. For example, full participation in the political process of our society is dependent on some proper knowledge and understanding of the recent history of this society and the world around it and of the scientific and technological issues and decisions facing it. A study of modern world history, a grounding in science and in the basis of technology are all therefore essential areas of knowledge. Other knowledge is required for more personal reasons, such as knowledge of options open to one in work and leisure and, at least, access to the specific knowledge required for a chosen field of activity. From arguments of this kind, we develop a framework for content that gives a rational, coherent and focused basis for selecting aspects of subjects and deciding whether and how to group them and what to make optional and compulsory. We describe the content using the following structure:

Three Areas of Knowledge and Understanding:
- Personal
- Social
- Scientific and Technological

Here most, but not all, of the current subject content would be remapped, with a slimmer nationally required core to be covered, with considerable scope for local and school choice in addition. The focus and aims for each part of the compulsory content will be clear so we will be free of nonsense such as the restriction of modern history to Key Stage 4 where it is optional and the arbitrariness of much of the current content.

The Experience of the Arts

Here all the arts would be included, and the appreciation of the built environment and natural beauty. In our view, the arts are not merely a different kind of knowledge but a qualitatively different area of experience . A coherent programme for arts education will develop important aesthetic, moral and human awareness alongside induction into major strands of our culture and of the pleasures of life.

Four Areas of Practical Competencies
- Communication and Numeracy
- Physical Movement and Health and Safety
- Social Interaction
- Planning and Organisation

Of course, these areas will principally be taught through other things but we believe that the profile of these aspects of practical learning should be raised. We need to move away from a narrow, and often decontextualised 'skills' approach to see that the development of competencies is the acquisition of significant skills alongside attitudes and knowledge. We cannot manage, let alone enjoy, our lives without these competencies and the proper use of them is fundamental to the social dimension of a self-determining life. Thus the competencies take their place as the third element of the content of the curriculum. There seems to me to be an enormous danger in the Dearing reforms of the current structure for cross-curricular work in health, careers and guidance, personal and social development, citizenship, etc., simply being lost. In the 1988 structure, these seemed very much afterthoughts and the guidance for mapping and recording work often over-elaborate and ponderous. Nonetheless, the cross-curricular elements provide a way of giving some meaningful links to the subject-based structure. It is, therefore, very much to be hoped that the near silence with which they are treated in Dearing does not lead to their disappearance in practice. Certainly, the government is quite wrong to suggest that the new Schools Curriculum and Assessment Authority (SCAA) model religious education syllabuses will ensure a moral education for our future citizens. Only a whole school approach to the curriculum, and not simply the content, can do that.

Content, in our view, is only part of the framework, since the institutional life of the school is also part of the whole curriculum, along with the structure for progression and the system for assessment. Some commentators have applauded the fact that the present National Curriculum leaves schools free to decide on their own ethos and values, although the NCC suggested that schools should be required to show what their core values are. In our analysis, this is not a satisfactory position and I will examine more closely the reasons why *the wider curriculum of the effective school* should be included in the framework of an adequate National Curriculum. We argue, from our essentially democratic position, that schools and individual teachers should have significant freedom of planning and curriculum decision returned to them. It is obviously vital that a school develops its own sense of community in partnership with its neighbourhood, parents and students, not least because it is at the level of school and local community that conflicting values in a pluralist and socially and ethnically diverse society can be weighed and prioritised. However, the current 'freedom' for schools to develop the 'whole curriculum' beyond the National Curriculum leaves a vacuum in place of a real entitlement. This will extend to values and attitudes as well as (apparently but falsely) value-free content. Certain principles and practices must pervade the whole curriculum of the school if access to the development of the personal qualities is to be guaranteed for all.

The second part of our framework, therefore, is a proposed requirement that all schools should draw up and publish policies for the following areas of school life which show how they aim to contribute to national and school aims:

- the whole curriculum plan
- the code of conduct
- the structure for partnership with students and families
- the involvement of the whole school community in decision-making
- the relationship with the local community
- the development of a social life and an extra-curricular programme
- the structures for promoting equal access to learning
- the establishment of interactive styles of teaching and learning
- opportunities for independent learning.

What we are raising here, particularly in the last two areas, is that a National Curriculum concerned with values and coherence needs to address issues of pedagogy as well as content. There is, of course, a strong link between the description of content in our framework and this second element because the practical competencies and, indeed, the relatedness of the areas of knowledge, understanding and the arts cannot be achieved without the support of an effective wider curriculum embedded in the life of the school.

A wider National Curriculum does not have to be a more prescriptive one. The third element of our framework is a *structure for progression and choice*. Each Key Stage should have a clear focus appropriate to the age and development of the students. At Key Stage 1, for example, this would focus on literacy and numeracy and the foundation of positive learning and social experience and be free from the present clutter of content that seems to be weakening literacy levels still further. Here I welcome what Dearing has had to say, although the worries of many infant and junior school teachers that the new focus on literacy, numeracy and information technology in Key Stages 1 and 2 could lead to poor skill-based practice, need to be taken seriously. This is a prime example of the way in which the details of what is in the statutory core, the precise wording of the statements of attainment and the style of tests that are developed will determine the effect of the broad policy. This could, and should, have been avoided by establishing the core aims. In our model for Key Stage 1, the establishment of a love of learning (a feature, of course, of all the best infant teaching) together with the development of co-operative as well as individual learning, would also be part of the 'foundation' focus.

I want to emphasise that a nationally set core programme of study should be just that: a core profile of work for each Key Stage with space for the school to add to it, to decide the structure for delivery and the context in which to set it. This would return to teachers the important role of detailed planning and contextualising the national agenda in the light of the needs and interests of their students. This is desirable both philosophically (on the basis of self-determination for teachers and the recognition of their professionalism) but also practically. The teacher is, if properly guided, supported and monitored, in the best position to know how to get the best from the students.

Choice should not, however, extend only to those planning and delivering the curriculum. There is no intrinsic conflict between an entitlement curriculum and guaranteed access to the major areas of learning, and real choice for students in their learning. On the contrary, the development of young people for a democratic society requires that they gain experience of making guided but significant choices. We identify four levels of possible student choice within the curriculum:

- within a given sequence of work, i.e., choice over the order;
- between options in a sequence of work, e.g., a compulsory core task, then choice between extension tasks;
- between options, where one of a variety of possibilities is required;
- between voluntary activities.

All Key Stages should include student choice at the first two and the fourth levels, which are, of course, extremely important as motivators and supports for active learning as well as providing experience of choice. We would want to extend the principle radically, supported by a modular structure of curriculum organisation, and argue that 15 per cent of the timetable at Key Stage 3 and 30 per cent at Key Stage 4 should be reserved for options.

At Key Stage 4, we envisage a largely modular structure involving vocational and academic learning and linked to a comprehensive post-16 structure. Here, too, there is a significant move towards the recognition of a potential place for vocational courses in the Dearing reforms which should be welcomed. Dearing has recognised the importance of creating space for school and pupil choice, but, because he has only constructed the curriculum in the blocks of subjects, he has achieved this by downgrading the place of the humanities and the arts. Whilst this may, paradoxically, be helpful for the future of single subject courses in the different subjects within these curriculum areas, it takes us a very long way away from the notion of an entitlement curriculum for all. This fact has led some to object to Dearing's reforms at this Key Stage on the grounds that he has effectively ended the National Curriculum at age 14. In our view of entitlement, the introduction of significant choice here is entirely appropriate, provided it is within a structure which guarantees access to the core of the whole and ensures that the choices interlink so that all routes taken lead, at least potentially, to the whole range of potential destinations. This is at risk because Dearing has not looked at the links with post-16 curriculum or the question of the place and nature of A-levels.

The current policies of restricting coursework to 20 per cent in most subjects at both GCSE and A level are not even mentioned in his report yet they enshrine a narrow model of academic learning that some GCSE and A level syllabuses had begun to widen quite dramatically, particularly those with modular structures. The current difficulties in establishing the right balance of knowledge and understanding with skills and practical ability in GNVQ syllabuses and criteria are no reason for abandoning the attempt to recognise a variety of styles of learning, and to give value to those other than the traditional academic model. Dearing has established a place for exploring this in Key Stage 4, but his language of separate pathways linked by bridges, set in the context of sharp differences of prestige, learning style and assessment pattern, is quite worrying.

At its worst, this approach will lead to low-level vocational courses for those who can only learn practically, with increasingly academic GCSE/A-level courses for those who can aspire to Higher Education or Further Education at least to intermediate level, something between 30 per cent and 60 per cent currently. In developing the details of the work Dearing has set out for SCAA and the National Council for Vocational Qualifications, this danger must be avoided at all costs. If realised, we will simply have a return to selection at 14 in place of that we abandoned at 11. The exclusion of 30–40 per cent of our future citizens from accepted educational success is no good at all for them or for the nation. Only a fully integrated system where all pathways link systematically, and all kinds of learning are valued, will meet the needs of our future citizens and our nation.

Finally, we come to the fourth and ultimately crucial part of the framework: *the system for assessment and recording.* By 1993 it was obvious to all but the government and its favoured education lobbyists, that the current National Curriculum Tests were likely to do enormous damage to the motivation of students and teachers and to cause a narrowing of the actual curriculum taught and a serious depression of the real standards achieved. In our analysis, this was because aims to do with enforcing the programmes of study, of monitoring and controlling teachers and schools and of driving for the return of selection have dominated the development of the tests and, even more, their implementation. The destructive imposed changes in GCSE, particularly with regard to coursework, the specification of tiered tests at Key Stages 3 and 4, the continuing policy shifts leading to the sacking of the agencies developing the tests, and the significant changes in the actual National Curriculum requirements and priorities written through the test specifications are all evidence of this. These were the educational reasons for the widespread support, within teaching and beyond, of the 1993 test boycott. The original purposes of the structure and approach to assessment of the National Curriculum—essentially to provide a clear measure of progress whilst ensuring continuity and progression for the individual pupil—had been left far behind in the drive for 'simple' tests that would provide a rigour said to be missing in the practice of most teachers. All arguments against the tests, and the league tables based solely on their results (thus dismissing teacher assessment altogether, as well as judging progress solely by what was testable in tests of this kind), were dismissed as a reluctance by teachers to let their work be measured. A very hostile view of the accountability of teachers was thus developed and imposed, as part of a wider thrust of policy to take away professional control of public services and establish so called consumer control through a market structure.

The situation in 1993 made it quite wrong to suggest that the two main pillars of the 1988 Education Reform Act—the Local Management of Schools and the National Curriculum—were working in opposite directions to achieve a constructive balance, whatever the original intention of HMI and others who contributed to their design. The reduction of the tests to simple and narrow exercises in memory and decontextualised abstraction pulls the whole National Curriculum to the side of encouraging a destructive and selective market in education where an educated elite of students are served well (if narrowly) by a well-resourced elite of academic schools. Neither the needs of the majority, nor of our society for a wide, deep and high standard of education for all future citizens will be served by this. In opposition to this approach, a huge consensus exists among industry, LEAs (including many under Conservative control), teachers, parents and educationalists to support the development of a unified system where academic and vocational courses run in parallel and where assessment records success and encourages high quality learning and continued education. In establishing parity of value for teacher assessment of pupils and external tests, in restricting (at least for the time being) the tests to English, Maths and Science, in making the tests far simpler and less narrow and rigidly tiered, Dearing has shifted policy very significantly back towards that consensus.

In 1993, Dearing succeeded in reassuring many outside the teaching profession that his reforms of the tests are sound and he has divided the teacher unions into those who will not undertake the recording of teacher assessment until the curriculum is slimmed down and the procedures are less onerous, and those who will not set, supervise or mark the tests but will do the required assessment until they are convinced that the slimming down and assessment arrangements are sound. Most significantly he has equated teacher accountability with the acceptance of external tests and external licensing (or auditing) of teachers to carry out the assessment of teachers. Teachers must, he believes, accept these external measures of the quality of their work in order to justify the control he wishes to give them over elements of the detail of what they teach, how they teach it, the context they provide for it and the way they assess and record the progress of their pupils.

This view of accountability appears wholly just and sound. It is, indeed, central to our argument for a national curriculum that education is too important for all to leave it simply in the hands of the few; the nation has a right to set the aims of education and to monitor the work of those professionals to whom it entrusts the task of implementing those aims. Even here, though, it is not that simple when the crucial decisions of detail are made out of the context of such strong aims. The nature and purpose of national tests and their relationship to teacher assessment is more problematic than Dearing recognises. Fewer, simpler and shorter tests are welcome in that their development shows a recognition that assessment is a secondary activity, even though it is essential to learning as well as to accountability and effective partnership with pupil and family. However, shorter tests and simpler record-keeping structures have the potential to do great damage. Simpler tests must, by and large, test the aspects of a subject that are easier to test: often specific, even discrete, elements of knowledge and isolated skills. It is possible to specify better simple tests which provide simulation style tasks to complete by drawing on prior knowledge and developed levels of understanding and skills. These, however, are not common forms of tests and not, for example, the type set out in the 1994 specification for Key Stage 3 English.

Whatever the value of conventional simple tests, they will not be able to measure the complex interrelationship of knowledge, understanding and skill that can be seen in sustained competence over a period of time. The best teacher assessment—whether GCSE coursework, BTEC identification of competences or in good departmental record keeping—does measure achievement in this way. The simple tests that Dearing will retain at Key Stages 1, 2 and 3 may help emphasise the importance of high levels of basic skills but will not measure the width of achievement that needs to be valued if we are to have a fully challenging and motivating curriculum. Above all, these tests will not be an adequate basis for moderating teacher assessment since quite different aspects of performance will be assessed. All systems for publication of results to parents, let alone the league tables still proposed for Key Stage 2, must combine the results of the tests and teacher assessment so that the full range of work of a pupil is presented. When both the tests and statutory record-keeping are married to the slimmed down curriculum and new statements of attainment, then we may see a very serious narrowing of focus as teachers teach to the skill-based core agenda by which they and their pupils are judged. At Key Stage 4, this process could lead to substantial streaming and setting as schools respond to the changes in GCSE and the new vocational courses in the ways discussed above. Such divisions at the top will, almost certainly, filter down the age range and the notion of a core entitlement for all will be further weakened. A fundamental look at the nature of the tests to be used, the framework for GCSE, and the way these will relate to the slimmed down subjects, as well as the structure for reporting, are all needed if Dearing's reforms in this area are to have positive results.

The problems in the assessment system, however, are not merely the hijacking by 1993 of the test development and specification by those committed ideologically to traditional pedagogy and selection. In our analysis, the single ten-level scale is a more fundamental obstacle to an adequate national curriculum. The existence of a single scale continuing across all Key Stages is bound to demotivate and frustrate the average and below, let alone those in special schools who remain, euphemistically, 'visiting' strands of Levels 1 and 2 for their entire school career. Such a scale of achievement, defined in terms of the content and potential attainments of a progressive and age-structured linear curriculum, is not the only way to guarantee a universal entitlement to a core curriculum. On the contrary, it often obstructs access to the level of content and skill required for maximum individual success by imposing the later programmes of study, pitched at high levels of skill and concept, on students still struggling with more basic levels of learning.

After considerable discussion in his interim report of these and other issues raised by the ten-level scale, Dearing proposed that it should remain up until the end of Key Stage 3, with GCSE and its existing nine letter grades being used for Key Stage 4. Dearing's main reason for retaining the ten levels is that he wishes to endorse the original TGAT aim of ensuring progression and continuity and that many people suggested in the consultation that the ten-level scale was helping both to do this and to raise standards. Importantly for Dearing, there was less concern and less consensus on this issue from schools, than on the other major issues raised in the consultation. All of this begs some very important questions. It was argued by Dearing in his interim report that the production of a single hierarchical scale was difficult in areas such as History or Geography where the orientation to knowledge makes it difficult to disentangle it from the achievement of skills or understanding. He went on to argue that this was less problematic in the core subjects of English, Maths, Science and Technology. This is a gross underestimation of the complexity of the relationship of these three dimensions of learning in all subjects and a failure to recognise that the order of development of all three differs between many, if not all, children.

This complexity and individuality of learning and progress can be recognised if we shift our focus to the establishment of clear standards of competence. These will set out, as do many of the current statements of attainment, criteria for demonstrating, in use, inter-related and applied knowledge and understanding and skills. The process by which such criteria are established, modified and then made accurate working tools for all teachers is a complex and expensive task. As Dearing stated in the interim report, the best criteria derive from the analysis of achievement of actual samples of work. Teachers can only learn these from their continuing involvement in well organised practice marking procedures. This is a dynamic process; criteria that are internalised by teachers inform the planning of work and can be set as targets for pupils whose quality of work improves, enabling more to reach the standard set. The mapping of what has been achieved against a predetermined hierarchy can often obscure completely both the actual achievement and the potential targets.

A better approach to assessment than the ten-level scale would be to establish proper standards of achievement in each strand of a subject based on the ability to use knowledge, skills and under-standing to demonstrate a given level of competence. We would cease to be concerned with hierarchies per se, let alone imagined pathways of development that infuse so many of the current statements. Rather, we would recognise that the quality of teaching and learning had risen when more pupils had achieved a given standard. We should establish the core standard in each subject (or area of the curriculum) and establish an adequate system of teacher assessment (supplemented by testing where this can measure achievement not easily recorded through ongoing work) to identify its achievement. In order to support differentiation, this core standard should be set in a profile indicating potential achievement from the programme of study at the core level and above and below it. The achievement of individual pupils would be reported on this profile to them and to their parents both within and at the end of each Key Stage. Nationally we would be able to measure the quality of our system against the core standards but without the unnecessary aggregation of achievement to a linear scale that would obscure rather than illuminate individual achieve-ment. An upper and lower band of the profile would allow a three-point scale to be used if this were felt necessary. Only at the end of

Key Stage 4 would it be necessary to divide achievement more finely by means of GCSE grades. As we achieve higher proportions of post-16 participation, however, even here we would need fewer grades and could report achievement in broader bands, with the use of a profile to give detailed information about the particular achievements of an individual. A national measure of quality should be in the achievement of the core standard by most, if not all.

These profiles should be set within a system based on redeveloped Records of Achievement and owned in partnership by school, student and family. Since a new profile would start with each Key Stage, building on the learning and achievement of the previous one but not carrying forward a summative level of achievement, this system offers better motivation to weaker students without reducing the challenge to the more able. The programme of study (including the Key Stage 3 and 4 options at a variety of levels) and the attainment profile would offer adequate differentiation to provide work at all levels of achievement with content and difficulty levels matched. The present resources now going into the development and administration of the tests, would be redirected to the production of standard assessment modules and moderation to validate the profiles. The original TGAT aims of integrating assessment into the normal teaching programme and validating practical as well as academic work would be restored without the disadvantages of the ten-level scale. This is an ambitious scheme but not beyond a nation that is willing to place its trust in the professionalism of its teachers to maintain fair and accurate records as the basis of assessment. Validation and moderation procedures would therefore be used to sample and check teacher assessment rather than to replace it or police every element. Such a model is well established and accepted as valid in much of vocational education and there is no reason why it cannot be developed reliably in a comprehensive school system.

I have now described all the elements of the alternative framework for an adequate national curriculum proposed by John White and myself in our IPPR paper. I have also rehearsed and updated our critique of the 1994 National Curriculum and argued that the case for root and branch rethinking remains despite the Dearing reforms. I want to close this chapter by considering one further issue. Since we have to work within the existing structure, which is now being changed to make more space for teacher and school adaptation and contextualisation, and our key task is to do our best by our students, what is the value of an alternative model to those of us working in schools now?

Arguing for radical change in the National Curriculum is not just a matter of intellectual purity nor an attempt to carve out a new ground for opposition to the government that we can occupy as educationalists. I believe that my critique of the 1994 National Curriculum shows that there remain grave dangers and damaging flaws and gaps in the structure and detail despite the welcome nature of many of the Dearing reforms. By setting out an adequate and coherent alternative we can show the kind of structure that is needed for personal and national success. The individual citizens of our nation need a broad and high level of education, preparing them for work in a highly developed and technological economy and for life in a complex and open society. Present policies, all too likely to involve a narrow statutory core, dominated by the need for simple tests or records, may reinforce failure and selection and the divide between the academic and the practical. This will not serve our national need at all. There is a potentially huge consensus across industry, politicians, parents and students for an adequate national education policy. This will have to include coherence and continuity in the curriculum, the right balance of the practical and the student-centred with the theoretical and the teacher-led, a proper validation of the achievements of the whole student and a clear structure of progression through and beyond compulsory schooling. As educationalists concerned with individual as well as national needs and success, we need to be ready to provide the detailed case for change. Dearing's great achievement has been to produce a welcome new respect for the views of teachers and yet the response of the unions to his reforms shows a lack of a clear shared alternative, as well as continued unease with the National Curriculum. For this reason alone it is urgent to open up the wider issues that the 1994 reforms too often miss.

In the meantime, we have to cope with the present. Drawing on our critique and alternative model, we can implement practical policies that create better coherence and progression. We can set the crude National Curriculum reporting firmly in a school based system that places the student, and family, at the centre of full records of achievement, offering formative feedback, target setting and motivation as well as levels. More ambitiously, we can work with regional consortia to validate core, wider and transferable achievements within the 14–19 curriculum. We can retain an active place for the arts and for social studies throughout the secondary curriculum and retain the maximum space for student choice. We can use resources under LMS to support extension and extra-curricular provision to offer the width and range of opportunities needed to maintain the confidence and success of all our students. By basing practical school-based policy on a fuller and more adequate view of the curriculum and of assessment, we are also drawing parents and students into a fuller understanding, based on actual experience, of a more coherent curriculum. If they see that a well-focused and more coherent model of learning and curriculum planning is available, they will be less tolerant of the narrowing and incoherent elements of the 1994 National Curriculum. Drawing now on an alternative model in order to do better by our present students is one of the most powerful ways of arguing for change. Sir Ron Dearing's greatest achievement in his 1994 reforms of the National Curriculum is to give us substantially more space in which to create that coherence in our schools and set the statutory core in a context of a positive view of our pupils and their learning and their potential. It is a space that I want to seize with alacrity.

5 AN INTERIM APPROACH TO UNIFYING THE POST-16 CURRICULUM

Michael Young, Annette Hayton, Ann Hodgson
and Andrew Morris

This chapter has two related concerns. One is substantive and concerned with the post-compulsory curriculum. The other is methodological and concerned with strategies for implementing alternative educational policies. The paper begins with the substantive issue of the growing crisis in the post-compulsory curriculum as more and more young people continue their full-time studies until 17 or 18 (or even later) in a system that was geared to the majority of them gaining employment. Following a brief review of policy in England and Wales for post-compulsory education in the last decade, we concentrate on the analysis developed in the Institute for Public Policy Research (IPPR) report *A British Baccalauréat* (Finegold et al., 1990). This report identified academic/vocational divisions as primarily responsible for the continued low levels of participation and achievement in post-compulsory education and argued quite explicitly for a unified system of qualifications for all post-16 students.

The paper goes on to question a form of analysis, such as that in the report, that calls for a unified system at the national level, when the government appears committed to perpetuating a divided system. This leads us to look beyond the national political context for an alternative basis for developing unifying strategies. In analysing current developments we identify the unifying possibilities, not at the national level but within current professional practice. We argue that this points to a need not only for a new understanding of the relationship between government policy and professional practice, but for the development of new relationships between *theory* (or the research and writing of those based in universities) and *practice*—the activities of those involved in delivering the curriculum in schools and colleges.[1] In the last section of the paper we describe an attempt which has taken its inspiration and aims from the IPPR report to develop such new relationships.

Post-Compulsory Education in England and Wales since the 1970s

Until the late 1980s there was no UK political party or pressure group which even claimed to have a distinctive policy for post-compulsory education and training. The provision that had emerged as a result of a number of piecemeal reforms, none of which had focused directly on the 16–19 age group, was fragmented and divided, and was characterised by low levels of participation and achievement. It was as if it were normal that nearly three out of every four young people should leave school as soon as it was legally possible. Even at the end of the 1970s, only about 30 per cent of 16-year-olds stayed on after the compulsory school leaving age and less than half of these went on to higher education.

What, in retrospect, is so striking now, is that such low levels of participation and achievement continued with little or no comment by professional groups or by politicians of the Right or the Left. Even among progressive and radical teachers who struggled to achieve comprehensive secondary schooling, there was little interest in post-compulsory education or how it might be reformed to include a wider section of the school population. The Sixth Forms of comprehensive schools were seen as little more than elitist left-overs of the grammar schools, and little if any attention was given to their curriculum or to what role they could play in a less exclusive system. Equally, there was little public interest in Further Education or the steady increase in numbers of Tertiary and Sixth Form Colleges. This was despite the fact that the Further Education colleges were responding to the drop in numbers of their traditional day-release students by taking a growing proportion of students on full-time A level courses.

The collapse of the youth labour market that began in the second half of the 1970s was the main catalyst for change in post-compulsory education. The first response by government was to fund a series of piecemeal initiatives for employer-based training which culminated in the New Training Initiative and the provision of a two-year youth training programme for all who left school at 16 (YTS). Parallel with this attempt to establish a viable work-based training scheme for young people, local education authorities developed a variety of 'prevocational' courses for the growing numbers staying on in school (or college) after 16. These courses recruited from those who had not done well enough to get on to an A level course but who were not keen to retake O levels (and later, GCSEs). Participation in full-time post-compulsory education grew steadily but not dramatically during the 1980s, and with A levels changing little, it led to the development of a growing diversity of low-level qualifications for what became known as *the new Further Education, and the new sixth form.*

The divisive and fragmented nature of educational provision from 16 onwards was highlighted by the Technical and Vocational Education Initiative (TVEI), which was launched in 1983 and made available to all secondary schools in 1986. This was a serious and, initially at least, well-funded attempt to provide a technical and vocational alternative to the narrow academic curriculum. It was explicitly a 14–18 programme designed to encourage more young people to complete a four-year course and it was the first national curriculum initiative to make equal opportunities with regard to race, gender and special educational needs an explicit criterion for funding. Evidence from the evaluations and elsewhere suggest that the outcomes of TVEI have been uneven. There is a record of much innovative and creative work, and special schools, in particular, have undoubtedly been able to broaden their curriculum offer through TVEI support. However, the combined effects of a deeply stratified society and a divided system of qualifications are enormous barriers to overcome. Ten years since the launch of TVEI, we have a picture of what might be called *internal change within a largely unchanging structure.* On the one hand, it is doubtful if we would have seen the developments such as flexible learning, more student-centred teaching, Recording Achievement, Individual Action Planning and the extensive use of IT if it had not been for TVEI. On the other hand, there are many features of 14–18 education which have changed little. For example:

- lack of continuity between 14–16 and 16–18 curricula;
- separate academic and vocational programmes with little if any possibilities of credit transfer;
- lack of communication between schools and colleges;
- diverse and competing forms of institutional delivery;
- competing examination boards;
- lack of co-ordination between government departments;
- a profound disvaluing of technical and practical studies.

The dominant role of A levels in post-16 education (even for those who did not take them), with their combined failure and drop out rate of 30 per cent, became even more evident with the entry of TVEI into Sixth Forms and colleges. TVEI funds supported a number of innovations designed to open up access to A levels and bridge the divide between them and vocational qualifications. However, even the best of such innovations (for example the Helix Project and the Wessex Scheme) never became more than local examples with national reputations. The only serious alternatives to A levels in the schools were the emerging prevocational programmes, for example the Certificate for Prevocational Education (CPVE). However, despite its innovative approach to pedagogy, the potential of CPVE was limited by the fact that it was part of a deeply divided system. All too easily prevocational programmes became one-year cul-de-sac courses with no clear progression to further study or employment.

For and Against a Unified System

In 1990, as an attempt to address some of the problems raised in the previous section, the report *A British Baccalauréat: Ending the Division Between Education and Training*, was published by the Institute for Public Policy Research (IPPR). The primary aim of the report, given that a General Election was expected in the next year, was to influence the thinking of the main political parties on post-compulsory education and training. It made a series of recommenda-tions which focused on the key role of academic/vocational divisions in limiting participation and achievement. The report was widely and very positively reported in the press; it was seen as presenting both a systematic analysis of current provision and a clear alternative. Since then, the IPPR report's argument for a unified system has become very much part of the professional consensus. This consensus became apparent in three important outcomes from the report which have relevance for the rest of this paper:

☐ The Royal Society in its report *Beyond GCSE* followed the IPPR recommendations almost exactly. This meant that the argument for a unified system was not restricted to the Left.

☐ Two follow-up conferences were held. One was at the Institute of Education in December 1991 in which six different professional organisations spoke in support of the British Baccalauréat proposals (Young and Watson 1992). The other was in Islington and brought together representatives of the local TEC, the CBI, as well as colleges and universities in London.

☐ As a result of a joint initiative with Islington LEA, the Post-16 Education Centre was given a grant by the Paul Hamlyn Foundation to explore ways of moving towards a more unified post-16 curriculum (Morris 1992).

As a result of the feasibility project, further funding was obtained from the Paul Hamlyn Foundation for what has become known as the Hamlyn Post-16 Unified Curriculum Project. This project, which involves the Post-16 Education Centre, Islington Federal College and Hackney Community College and CILNTEC (the Central and Inner London North Training and Enterprise Council) and which began in May 1993 will be discussed in the last section of this paper.

Of far greater significance than any of these developments, however, were two national events and a social change which have together transformed the context for post-compulsory education in this country. The first national event was the publication, in May 1991, of the White Paper *Education and Training for the 21st Century*. It was clearly influenced by the IPPR report's argument for a unified system as well as by the Labour Party's support for a weaker (and soon forgotten) version of an advanced diploma. Launched in a pre-election year, the White Paper was a clever combination of *progressive* and *regressive elements*. The most obvious progressive policies were:

☐ the first attempt, through the NVQ levels, to establish a national qualification framework;

☐ the official (albeit somewhat rhetorical) commitment to parity of esteem between academic and vocational qualifications;

☐ the launching of a new 'independent' FE sector which was welcomed by nearly all those professionally involved in Further Education

☐ the unifying (or nearly so) of higher education, by allowing all polytechnics and a number of colleges to become universities;

☐ the announcement of two overarching Diplomas for 16–19 year olds (though virtually nothing has been heard of them since).

The three *regressive* policies were:

☐ the consolidation of a divided curriculum by establishing a new kind of general vocational qualification (GNVQs) rather than diversifying the existing academic route and thus developing a single system;

☐ the separation of general and vocational adult education with regard to funding;

☐ the restriction of the amount of coursework allowed in the assessment of A levels (and GCSE), thus limiting the possibilities for students to move between academic and vocational courses.

The second significant event was the Conservative Party's victory in the General Election in April 1992. This confirmed that we had a government that was firmly committed to retaining A levels (and therefore opposed to developing a more unified system of qualifications). However, the Employment Department, at least the sections responsible for TVEI, has kept open options for a more unified approach. There are signs also, in the SEAC (School Examinations and Assessment Council—now Schools Curriculum and Assessment Authority) announcement on modular A levels, that a more flexible position on the post-16 curriculum may be emerging.

The social change that is transforming the post-compulsory sector and creating quite new problems for government policy is the much faster rise in the 16+ staying-on rate from 1990 onwards. By 1993 this had reached 67 per cent nationally (varying between nearly 50 per cent and over 80 per cent in different parts of the country). Increases in staying on after 17 are much smaller and by 18 only 35 per cent remain in full-time education. We still have, therefore, a deeply divided system, dominated by provision for the top 20–30 per cent of those who take GCSE, which is not well suited to cope with the higher levels of participation of the 1990s. In other words, despite substantially higher levels of participation in full-time education after 16, the problem of low levels of achievement remains. The argument made in the IPPR report and elsewhere (Young 1993) is that it is simply not possible in the UK (though this is clearly not true in all other countries) to build high levels of achievement for the school population *as a whole*, on the basis of a divided system. However, though the basic analysis which was developed in 1990 in the IPPR report is no less applicable in 1993, the political and social context is very different. It follows that the strategies that are needed for achieving a high performance system may also be different.

78

We have stressed the General Election result for two reasons. First, the IPPR report was clearly geared to the election of a new Labour or coalition government. Second, in funding a project for unifying the post-16 curriculum, the Paul Hamlyn Foundation envisaged that it would be supporting a *national policy* geared to achieving a unified system. The reality has of course been very different; unification, at least in the form envisaged in the IPPR report, is not currently on the national agenda, despite the growing professional consensus, but the support from industry (CBI 1993) for a unified system is undoubtedly stronger. It is this new reality and the possibilities it may offer which the next section of the paper turns to.

1993 and Beyond

In this section we review the conditions for a unified system, the tendencies that, despite overt government policies in favour of maintaining divisions, point towards unifying policies, and the unintended outcomes of policies that may also point in this direction. Together they indicate a need for some revision of the approach to educational policies adopted in the IPPR report, and to a rather different strategy to that which the report implied.

The case for a national unified system for post-16 education that was made in the IPPR report undoubtedly remains strong (Young and Watson 1992). It is significant to contrast the recent CBI report 'Routes for Success' (CBI 1993) with their earlier and highly influential, though more anodyne 'Towards a Skills Revolution' (1989). In 'Routes for Success' the CBI supports many of the arguments for a unified system in which students can transfer credit and move easily between different kinds of qualifications and modes of study. Though couched in rather different terms to the IPPR report, it is an indication of the extent to which arguments for a unified system have been accepted by those not directly involved in education. However, despite this growing consensus on the need for a unified system, the political reality is that the *primary conditions* for such a change are not present. *Four* conditions would seem to be necessary, of which only, at best, the first two (which are arguably not the most important) are in place:

(i) A *widespread professional consensus that*:
   ● a unified system is the only way to achieve genuine parity of

esteem between academic and vocational qualifications;

- a policy of encouraging institutional co-operation is both necessary and desirable;
- access routes to higher education other than with A levels are normal rather than the exception;

(ii) a view of the importance of continuing education and training *for the whole population* that is endorsed by both sides of industry and commerce;

(iii) sufficient political will on the part of government to introduce a unified system despite the opposition of influential interest groups;

(iv) the emergence of post-compulsory education as a popular issue (in the sense of being a high priority among voters) that might (like the poll tax, or perhaps testing) put pressure on a government with a small majority.

Although our conclusions about the political conditions for unification are pessimistic, when we turn from political analysis to economic considerations, there are grounds for suggesting that the pressures for change will become stronger. Most analyses of the continuing crisis in our economy suggest that economic opportunities in the next century will demand not only higher overall levels of skill and knowledge but increasingly flexible responses to change at an individual and institutional level. Such analyses make radical suggestions for the restructuring of industrial organisations in terms of flat hierarchies, the need for polyvalent (or multi-skilled) workers, and collaborative competition. The educational implications of such analyses have yet to be developed, but it is clear that they will mean far more than a quantitative leap in participation and levels of achievement.

Such changes in industrial reorganisation have direct implications for education and require a complete rethinking of the role of learners and teachers as well as the form that educational organisations should take. What is new is not just the changes themselves but that if higher performance in the system as a whole is to be achieved, these changes will need to apply to every school and college and all their departments, units and teams within them. For example, each unit or department will have to:

- make explicit how its activities are related to the aims of increasing achievement;
- be aware of how it relates to the aims of the school or college

as a whole;
- see *itself* as a proactive agent of change.

Expressed in the language of the new management theory, each section of a school or college will itself have to become a *learning organisation*. The last section of this paper will develop this argument by drawing on the recent experiences of the Post-16 Education Centre and its collaboration with post-16 providers in Hackney and Islington to give some illustrations of what such an approach might mean in practice. Before that, however, some reassessment of both the changing context of post-16 education and the analysis and strategy presented in the IPPR report is necessary.

The National System and Beyond; Unifying Tendencies and Policies with Unifying Potential

The IPPR report argued that the national system of institutions and qualifications for post-compulsory education remains dominated by divisions—between schools and colleges, between full- and part-time students, and between types of qualifications, to name but three. However if we look at what is happening on the ground, we can see that another picture is emerging of forces working against those divisions. There are a number of *tendencies* (not a direct product of any policy) and a number of unintended consequences of policies that are working against the divisions and could provide the material and practical conditions for a more unified system. There is evidence, for example, of what we could call *changes in the culture*:

☐ *Increased voluntary staying-on after 16*
This means that the cohorts of young people at 16+ are becoming less divided between those in employment and those in full-time study. Furthermore, it suggests that continuing in full-time education is becoming less tied to social class even if this weakening of social class differences has yet to make its appearance in access to higher education.

☐ *A greater awareness among young people and their parents of the importance of getting qualifications and their relationship to employment possibilities*
This is a slow but direct result of the disappearance of the youth labour market.

☐ *The expansion, greater diversity and accessibility of higher education*
This is taking a number of forms and begins to make university education appear less exclusive and beyond the reach of all but a few:

- The growing number of alternatives (in both older and new universities) to the single subject honours degree;
- The extension of university status to nearly all institutions of higher education;
- The growing proportion of degrees that are offered outside universities by institutions not previously associated with higher education.

☐ *A greater awareness of international comparisons*
This has meant that people have additional external criteria by which to judge national policies and their outcomes.

☐ *The rising skill levels of jobs*
As a result of skill audits carried out by Training and Enterprise Councils, more employers are becoming aware that an increasing number of the new jobs being created are for people with at least university entrance-level qualifications.

These tendencies are an indication that, despite continuing divisions within the qualification structure, changes in the economy are providing powerful pressures towards greater unity and flexibility.

This argument about pressures against old divisions is given greater strength if we turn to some of the actual policies initiated in recent years. Many policies directed at the 14–18 age group can be described as attempts to *encourage participation and achievement within a divided system*. Working within this contradiction, it is not surprising that teachers have been able to turn such policies towards ends for which they were not always envisaged. We describe this process as the *unifying potential* within policy developments which was a powerful feature of TVEI in the 1980s. The term *potential* is used because any *unifying outcomes* will depend not only on how teachers and others interpret the policies but on the broader political purposes of which they are a part (Young 1993). Realising the unifying potential of specific policies or practices depends on how they can move beyond their piecemeal and ad hoc origins and become part of a national strategy. Examples of this kind of policy with unifying potential are:

- records of achievement
- individual action planning
- more integrated approaches to guidance and counselling
- new modes of learner-centred assessment
- more flexible modular general vocational qualifications
- modular A and AS levels

Before considering the role of such policies in a new approach to unification, the next sections of the paper reconsider aspects of the analysis in the IPPR report in light of the changed context.

The British Baccalauréat Analysis Reconsidered

The Changing Context

The changed political conditions and the evidence of unifying tendencies described in the previous sections suggest that viewing unification primarily in terms of the alternative between unified or divided national systems may not be the most strategic approach, at least in the current circumstances. If a new strategy is to build more effectively on the professional consensus and support from employers, more weight needs to be given to the role of professional practice and local initiatives in the process of change.

The IPPR authors fully recognised their intellectual debt to practitioners; indeed it is doubtful if *A British Baccalauréat* could have been written if there had been no Wessex Modular Scheme. However, with its priority of influencing the national political debate, the report gave little attention to how its ideas for a unified system might work back into professional practice. This is particularly apparent in the lack of attention given to the question of implementation. By implication, there was an assumption that a unified system could be the result of a government edict, rather than through a complex partnership between national government and the variety of professional and other interests involved. Before developing this point further in relation to the current context, it is worth summarising the main arguments in the IPPR report. The analysis brought together three elements as follows:

☐ *professional dissatisfaction with the inflexibility and divisive character of the present system*

Teachers realised that students did not neatly fit into academic and vocational tracks, and that therefore such tracking unnecessarily inhibited learning and motivation.

☐ *analyses of the relationship between a divided qualifications system and local labour markets*
Research by David Raffe has shown how the aspirations of students and their incentives to study are lowered by a divided qualifications system.

☐ *the global economic argument about the need to move from a 'low-skills' to a 'high-skills' equilibrium*
The IPPR report was deeply influenced by the work of Finegold and Soskice (1988) which highlighted the discrepancy between new skill demands and the education and training *system* in this country.

These strands of analysis have not been seriously challenged. However, the report failed to be explicit about the process of implementation and could not take account of the changing political context and therefore of the need for new strategies for the 1990s.

Gaps in the Original British Baccalauréat Analysis

As suggested earlier, the pre-election context in which the IPPR report was published meant that a stress on national policies (inevitably of a top/down kind) was not surprising. It was no less surprising that the issue of implementation, and therefore the role of practitioners, was neglected. However, the issue is deeper than the need to respond to a changed political context or even the neglect of the process of policy implementation. It reflects major changes in the significance of national policies and, at a more theoretical level, an increasingly inadequate model of the education system. The next section of the paper considers two issues: (i) differing views of the role of professional practice in educational policy changes; and (ii) whether or not educational policy is seen primarily in terms of replacing one national policy with another. It argues that each is best understood in terms of the model we have of the education *system*.

Theoretically, we can identify an *old* concept of a system as like an organism and as having its antecedents in physiological analogies. The structural features of such a model of a system are that: (i) like organisms they are geared to survival; and (ii) 'direction', or purpose, is externally imposed on the parts—the body by the brain, the factory by the management, the school by the headteacher, and the society by the government. In a global context of increasing uncertainty more flexible responses are required at all levels. This suggests that a model of system in which direction and purpose are defined externally from above may be increasingly inappropriate. A new concept of system may be necessary in which purpose and direction are interdependent and *internal to the parts*—parts may be regions, localities or institutions when referring to a nation, or teams, units or departments when referring to a school or college.

This rather general analysis can usefully be extended to educational policy. Within the *old* idea of a system, policy changes are defined largely in terms of national policy. Likewise, critiques and alternatives (i.e. new policies) are limited by the assumption that change is invariably top/down. Furthermore, old system perspectives, whether of the Right, the Centre or the Left, are desensitised to the change-potential for the system as a whole of new practices that emerge at levels and in contexts other than that of management in the case of institutions, and government in the case of nation-states. In *old system* terms, particularly for those on the Left, localised or institution-based forms of change are often viewed as irrelevant or even as examples of co-option into the status quo. From this perspective, the only changes that count are the 'whole system' changes. However, the fact that the tendencies and practices which we have identified as having unifying potential do not originate in opposition to government policy may be their strength rather than their weakness. Whereas 'surviving' in physiological terms means keeping the existing system intact despite temporary threats (such as illnesses), surviving in the new global context will depend on how quickly institutions (or nation-states) can adapt to changes in the wider context. Such adaptation will not just rely on new national policies, but will involve *all parts of the system* embodying a sense of 'direction' and taking account of possible futures.

The issue that remains, of course, is whether incremental changes at the local or institutional level, such as those we have referred to, are just another example of the old English capacity for fragmented and localised innovation *without change*. The assumption of this paper is that they are both necessary for and can be the basis for real structural change towards a more democratic system of post-compulsory education. In the final section, we will return to the issue of what might be necessary for the potential of local innovations to be fully realised.

This requires replacing the old system metaphor of an organism that has dominated so much social science as well as educational policy, with a new, *connective* model of a system in which the metaphors are from neurology and holography.

Connectivity as a Metaphor for a Reformed 16-19 System

The previous section suggested that an educational strategy based on a new concept of system will be necessary if the current unifying tendencies and those practices identified as having unifying potential are to become elements of a unified system. In suggesting that the idea of connectivity should replace the ideas of *machine and organism* as the guiding system metaphor (Young 1994; Spours and Young 1992), the key distinction is in the location of purpose and direction. In a machine purpose and direction are external (in the mind of the designer and owner) and in the traditional concept of organism purpose is external to the parts and in a passive relationship to the environment. In a connective system, the purpose of the whole is expressed *in the parts and their inter-relationships*. In the case of the education system, this would imply that when a change was initiated in a part of the system, it would need to be seen in terms of how it expressed elements, within itself, of the overall purposes of the whole system; similarly, if a change is initiated as national policy, the question to be asked would be how such a change would be expressed at the institutional and team or department level. For example, the implementation of the National Record of Achievement or the development of a credit transfer scheme would need to be understood, not just in terms of whether every institution was using it, but whether it was improving progression at 16+ and 18+.

Institutions and Connectivity

The most familiar ideas associated with the concept of connectivity or of a connective system are networks and flat hierarchies. They derive from organisational theory (Morgan 1988) and are designed to contrast new organisational forms with those based on traditional bureaucratic hierarchies. However, such a polarising of alternatives has its dangers. It may be adequate for describing community groups or co-operatives and certain forms of user networks, but it has only limited applicability in the case of educational organisations involved in structural change.

Connectivity can take both horizontal (the focus on sub-part or intra-sector relationships) and vertical (part-to-whole and inter-sector relationships) forms. Furthermore, in relation to education, it can be applied both to organisational structures and to the curriculum. Organisational connectivity, therefore, takes horizontal forms such as the emerging examples of school–school and school–college collaboration and can extend to the kind of regional networks that will be described later in the paper. It can also take vertical forms represented by the emerging relationships between colleges, schools and universities. What distinguishes these new forms of system from the old—in particular, those associated with local educational authorities, for example, the system of Tertiary Education Boards in the ILEA—is that they arise internally from the needs and initiatives of the schools and colleges and are not external to them or imposed on them. Emphasising this difference between the internal and external origins of old and new systems is not of course to deny that a new system cannot be catalysed externally. The examples of connective system that we describe in the last section arose from the opportunity provided by external funding.

Curriculum and Connectivity

The idea of connectivity applied to the curriculum is illustrated in the growing number of attempts to articulate for learners a sense of the curriculum as a set of connections that cross subject, institutional and sector boundaries, and thereby help them to relate their learning to their experiences and their possible future. Its most ambitious forms are found in the various examples of learning frameworks (for example, that initiated at Wirral Metropolitan College) and the use of systems of credit accumulation and transfer that are emerging at national and regional levels, as with, for example, the London Together Initiative. All such attempts will involve establishing new bases of consensus among practitioners in relation to, for example, module design, credit equivalences, common assessment and guidance criteria and credit transfer.

The next sections of this paper are an attempt to illustrate these rather abstract ideas in the case of a project that we are involved in.

Towards Connectivity

We referred earlier in the paper to the fact that the Hamlyn Post-16 Unified Curriculum Project had its intellectual origins in the IPPR proposals for a British Baccalauréat. The decision to base the project in the Post-16 Education Centre, though partly by chance, also reflected the broad agreement of those working in the Centre with the policy recommendations of the IPPR report. Furthermore, the idea of bringing theory and practice together, and the forms of collaboration which the project developed in its feasibility phase, owed a great deal to the existing working methods of the Post-16 Education Centre, and a particular view of the relation between theory, or research, and practice. This section begins by describing the rationale of some of the Post-16 Education Centre's other activities and how they have influenced the project's approach before moving on to describing the beginnings of the project itself.

Networking Activities: The Background

From 1987 to 1991 the Post-16 Education Centre was funded by the Department of Employment to support and disseminate work arising from TVEI. Its work has included a range of activities which set out to overcome some of the divisions between practitioners in schools and colleges, whose main concern is effective *practice* within their institutions, and those in universities concerned with policy analysis and research. However, these activities were rooted in a model of change which saw its main function as *dissemination* of previously developed ideas about strategy and policy.

The extension of dissemination into dialogue began through our involvement with the London Region Post-16 TVEI Network. This was formed in 1989 with the aim of exchanging information about developments in post-16 education among the 32 London boroughs. Activities such as local events and conferences are organised through the Network planning group which comprises institute staff and co-ordinators of TVEI projects. This group affords a real opportunity for dialogue between practice-based and theory-based group members. It was experience of this type of collaboration with practitioners that the Post-16 Education Centre brought to the feasibility phase of the Hamlyn Post-16 Unified Curriculum Project and which has informed current research and development work.

The Centre now employs a number of strategies which are designed to promote more interactive links between theory and practice. These links have two related aims. First, the Centre wants its research and policy analysis to be grounded in the experience and understandings of practitioners who have the responsibility for the day-to-day delivery of policy. Second, it wants to extend the policy analysis and research capacities of practitioners to provide a collective resource for schools and colleges. In the terms of the earlier discussion about *old* and *new* concepts of system, the Centre has tried to replace the dependency and separation that have too often characterised the relationships between universities and schools/colleges with forms of connectivity and interdependence that recognise the different roles and build on them.

The Hamlyn Post-16 Unified Curriculum Project

The Hamlyn Post-16 Unified Curriculum Project (UCP) attempts to express the idea of connectivity in its aims, in its methodology and in its management. Its substantive concerns are to develop unifying strategies to raise levels of participation and achievement in post-16 education and training in Hackney, Islington and the City of London and to contribute to a national strategy for unifying the post-16 curriculum. It therefore has a national as well as a local focus and is a practical development project as well as a research project.

In both its development work and its research, the UCP aims to develop and evaluate unifying strategies which work against the divisions that have evolved within post-16 education and training. It starts with the assumption that in the present context unifying strategies are likely to be most effective if they begin at the local and regional level. However, it is also a national project, and those involved do not assume that the project area can or should be seen in isolation. The national focus of the project's aims is expressed in two ways. First, the research base in the Post-16 Education Centre will ensure that a body of evidence is built up which will contribute to the national policy debate. Second, the project is closely connected through working group membership to a number of complementary initiatives that are developing elsewhere, both nationally and regionally.

The project is designed to promote connectivity in a number of ways. For example:

- for individual learners—between learning elements that lie in the different academic, vocational and general tracks;
- for teachers—between teaching styles and models of assessment designed for learners in the different tracks;
- for institutional managers—between the resourcing, timetabling and guidance procedures associated with each track;
- for local institutional consortia—between the institutions that specialise in providing for different tracks (e.g., schools and colleges);
- for those involved in guidance—between the various ways of helping learners to achieve progression goals;
- for researchers and teachers—between the practical (or developmental) needs of the project and its research (or theoretical) needs.

The assumption implicit in the IPPR report 'A British Baccalauréat' was that these forms of connectivity would flow from a central, government-led reform of the 18+ qualification system—the replacement of academic and vocational qualifications by a single Advanced Diploma. In contrast to this view, the UCP is exploring the unifying potential of 'bottom-up' measures. Initially four main strategies have been selected not only because it is hoped that they will contribute to a broader unifying strategy, but because they respond to the immediate needs of the institutions involved. They are:

Modularisation of the Curriculum

Implementation will be through the development of modules which bridge the academic/vocational divide, which can be delivered in different institutional settings and which will be accessible to a wide variety of learners.

The Use of a Credit Framework

The focus will be closely related to the programme of modularisation and will be based on the Further Education Unit's proposals in 'A Basis for Credit'.

Introduction of GNVQs

The potential of GNVQs, and particularly the optional units, will be explored for their unifying potential both in relation to A levels and GCSEs and NVQ work-based programmes.

Progression Arrangements

The focus will be on facilitating learner movement and encouraging learners to transfer between different sectors and levels of education and training.

In pursuit of these four strategies, sub-project proposals have been invited from teachers, lecturers, trainers and others across institutions in the Hackney, Islington and City area of London. About fifteen proposals have been agreed. Those concerned with modularisation and attaching credit value cover the following areas:

- a European dimension in GNVQs
- careers education
- maths for future engineers
- enhancing core skills in GNVQs
- providing supplementary skills for disadvantaged students

Other projects will look at developing a format for specifying the full requirements for entry to a course or module, exploring the potential of using credits for admissions to higher education, and developing a system for exchanging accredited modules and associated learning materials between institutions using the Open College Network.

The management and support of these developments is collaborative. Detailed decision-making about the development of the project takes place through a local working group. This group comprises curriculum planners from Further Education Colleges, Sixth Form centres, adult education and youth training, together with representatives of the Institute of Education and the local TEC. This group is exploring how to resolve differences between institutions in different sectors, and attempting to integrate the activities of the many sub-projects, as well as examining how the research and development parts of the project can complement each other.

Connectivity between the research and development aspects of the project involves combining the formative (supporting practitioners), evaluative (providing evidence of outcomes) and developmental (contributing to national and local strategies) aspects of the research, as well as making sure that the dialogue between research and practice is two-way. We shall aim to achieve this connectivity in the following ways:

- regular feedback to the development projects from the evaluation;

- a series of seminars for all those involved with others researching and developing related national initiatives;
- local and regional dissemination of project working papers.

Conclusions

This paper has described a shift from *division* to *connectivity* in three related senses—one substantive and two methodological. Substantively, it has been concerned with developing post-compulsory curricula that overcome academic/vocational divisions and emphasise the interdependence of theoretical and practical studies, of different knowledge areas, and between different kinds of providers. We have used the term connectivity rather than unification on the grounds that the kind of unity likely to be realised in the future will not be imposed from above but will arise through sets of connections that start from below and are both horizontal and vertical. Methodologically the paper has focused primarily on the issue of overcoming the division between theory and practice and developing a more connective model of the relationship between the research activities and the practical delivery of curricula. It has also tried to examine what is involved in the process of change towards a more coherent and unified system of post-compulsory education in a context in which government policy is devoted to allowing the market to accentuate divisions and fragmentation. In such a context, the only option is the development of 'bottom-up' forms of system at the institutional, regional and national levels which we describe as connective.

We have argued that connectivity can be both horizontal (in the familiar sense of networks) and vertical (typically found in education as HE or education/business compacts). However, whether connectivity occurs within institutions or within regions, nationally or internationally, real connectivity between the parts depends on political decisions to establish connectivity in the system as a whole. This depends on a clear and realistic vision of the future. The argument of this paper is that in the circumstances we are likely to face in the next century, any vision for a more equitable or more efficient system of post-16 education must be a unified one. It must also be dependent on a powerful sense of connectivity in the system as a whole. The project that we describe and which is just beginning is, we hope, a small step to generating that connectivity in one sector of education in Britain.

6 TEACHER EDUCATION AND TEACHER COMPETENCE

Pat Mahony and Geoff Whitty

Even if the New Right's aim of a total transfer of teacher training out of higher education into the schools is not realised, it now seems likely that the nature of teacher education will be transformed out of all recognition in the next few years. Many changes have already taken place. Even before Kenneth Clarke, as Secretary of State for Education and Science, proposed making some courses 80 per cent school-based (DES 1992), conventional full-time four-year undergraduate courses (BEd/BA QTS) and one-year postgraduate (PGCE) courses had been joined by a variety of shortened and extended courses, part-time courses, and by the new school-based articled and licensed teacher schemes (Whitty et al., 1992; Barrett et al., 1992). We also had an incipient national curriculum for teacher education, in the form of the Secretary of State's criteria administered by the Council for the Accreditation of Teacher Education (CATE), long before the school system had one. Yet, until recently, it could have been argued that the changes had so far been less than apocalyptic (O'Keeffe 1990a).

However, the announcement that there was to be a pilot school-centred training scheme for 250 teachers with funding going directly to schools rather than higher education was a clear signal of the Major government's ultimate intentions for teacher education as a whole (Pyke 1993). That was followed by a 'blue paper' (DFE 1993a) and an Education Bill which proposed to move the funding of teacher education in England away from the Higher Education Funding Council (HEFCE) and transfer it to a new Teacher Training Agency more directly under the control of the Secretary of State.

Meanwhile, as we contemplate the new circular on primary training (DFE 1993c) and prepare for 66 per cent school-based secondary PGCE courses in response to John Patten's modifications of the Clarke proposals (DFE 1992), some initial indications of the effects of these policies are already being felt. The requirement that all

PGCE secondary courses should transfer some of their income to schools is making it difficult for some higher education institutions to maintain a role in initial teacher education even before the new school-centred scheme has made an impact (Sidgwick, Mahony and Hextall 1993).

Furthermore, the original version of the circular that will extend the government's reforms into primary training contained a direct threat to the notion of teaching as a graduate profession (DFE 1993b). Even though the proposal for a one-year training for non-graduate early years specialists was dropped in the final version of the primary circular, it is difficult to maintain a sanguine attitude about the future. As Stuart Maclure put it:

> The thing to remember about Government plans for teacher training is that there is a plot and a sub-plot. The plot is straightforward. Give practising teachers a bigger part to play in the professional preparation of their future colleagues. This is a good idea....The sub-plot is more sinister. It is to take teacher training out of the universities and colleges and ultimately to sever the connection between the study of education in higher education and its practice in schools. This is a deeply damaging idea and must be fought tooth and nail...the [government's policies] must be examined closely for insidious attempts to dismantle the traditional defences of teaching as a profession (Maclure 1993).

The proposals contained in the 1993 Bill confirm these suspicions and would give enormous powers to the Secretary of State and the Teacher Training Agency to encourage school-centred and school-provided schemes of training, to decide on the funding and location of student numbers, to accredit courses (following the abolition of CATE), and even to control research funding relating to teacher education. In these circumstances, even if higher education retains a role in teacher education, it is likely to be on condition that it fully supports the government's approach.

Education Reform and Teacher Education Reform

Since teacher education is still in the process of being restructured, it is not easy at this stage to judge whether these reforms will turn out to be more or less intense than the government's policies for schools.

What is clear is that there are some interesting parallels. Circular 3/84 (DES 1984), which established CATE, can be seen as part of the broader political and educational project of the Thatcher government (Whitty et al. 1987). It had significant material and ideological effects on the nature of teacher education at institutional level, although different teacher education institutions displayed differential wills and capacities to resist (Barton et al. 1992). Some institutions basically did CATE's bidding regardless of their own beliefs, others found ways of preserving most of their existing practices albeit sometimes under new labels, while a few took the CATE exercise as an opportunity to rethink their work in a positive manner. The policy-in-use has thus looked rather different and far less monolithic in its effects than any analysis of the official policy texts might have suggested. There are obvious parallels here with the analyses of the implementation of the National Curriculum in schools carried out by Stephen Ball and Richard Bowe (Ball and Bowe 1992).

Another parallel with school-level reforms lies in the apparent inconsistencies in government policy. Many commentators have pointed to the irony in the contrast between the stringent requirements imposed by CATE on award-bearing initial training routes and the deregulation implied by the creation of what Ted Wragg has called an 'el cheapo' licensed teacher route to Qualified Teacher Status (QTS) that does not require CATE approval (Reid and Newby 1988; Lawton 1990). In some ways, this parallels the tension between a centrally prescribed National Curriculum for schools, on the one hand, and the market-oriented approach of much of the rest of the Education Reform Act, such as open enrolment and local management, on the other (Whitty 1989).

The New Right and Teacher Education

Obviously, government policy in a liberal democracy derives from whole variety of influences, opportunities and constraints, and it would be a mistake to see it as entirely driven by clearly articulated ideological positions. However, under the Thatcher government, various New Right think-tanks *did* have considerable influence. It has now become commonplace to identify two main strands within New Right thinking—namely neo-liberal and neo-conservative. Andrew Gamble argues that what was distinctive about Thatcherism as a force within British Conservatism was its capacity to link the neo-conservative emphasis on tradition, authority and national identity with the application of neo-liberal free market economics to whole new areas of social activity (Gamble 1993). In doing this, Thatcherite policies entailed a strange combination of centralised state control and the encouragement of market forces.

In teacher education, as elsewhere, New Right pressure groups of both persuasions have been at work in recent years, seeking to influence policy. A spate of newspaper columns and pamphlets going back at least to the late 1970s has served to undermine confidence in teacher education institutions and prepare the ground for reform (Dawson 1981; O'Hear 1988; Hillgate Group 1989; O'Keeffe 1990b; Lawlor 1990). The protagonists have generally been agreed that there is something rotten about the current condition of teacher education, though they vary somewhat in their diagnoses and suggested solutions. Amongst their various arguments are that initial teacher training courses:

- place too little emphasis on the learning of subject knowledge
- place too little emphasis on classroom skills
- place too much emphasis on educational theory
- emphasise the wrong type of theory
- emphasise trivia
- are obsessed with race and inequality
- are informed by a spurious neo-Marxist view of culture
- produce students who have no respect for traditional values
- are too expensive
- are ineffective.

That the New Right's concern has been an ideological one, not merely a cost-saving exercise, was made clear in a very early attack on the sociology of education:

> Sociology of education should be cut out of courses for student teachers, not primarily as a means of reducing the Public Sector Borrowing Requirement (important though that is) but to improve the intellectual and moral environment in which would-be teachers are taught (Dawson 1981, p.60).

Dawson's view was that sociology, which 'started out by being harmless but ineffectual...is no longer harmless either'. The claim that teacher training is harmful has subsequently been broadened well beyond the sociology of education. For example, Anthony O'Hear made a rather crass connection between the academic success of the leading independent schools and their supposed tendency to employ untrained graduates as teachers (O'Hear 1988). The point has recently been repeated in a leading article in the *Spectator*:

> Anyone who wants to teach in a state school in this country must by law hold a qualification from an establishment approved for teacher training. The state sector includes the worst schools in the land, in terms of the quality of the product they turn out. Anyone who wishes to teach in a private school in this country can be admitted to the teaching staff at the discretion of the head teacher, irrespective of that person's qualifications. The private sector includes the best schools in the land, in terms of the quality of the product they turn out. It appears at last to be dawning on this Government, after 14 years in office, that these two points are linked (27 February 1993, p.5).

Both O'Hear and the *Spectator* editorial imply that teacher training courses actually diminish the effectiveness of teachers. Thus, the *Spectator* suggests that 'the dismal results many public-sector teachers...achieve for their pupils', despite their elaborate training, can quite reasonably be attributed to the poor quality and ideological bias of that training. Such simplistic conclusions tempt us to suggest that, far from removing sociology of education from teacher training courses, it might be helpful to introduce it into the training of philosophers and periodical leader writers, particularly if (like O'Hear) they are subsequently to become members of CATE. Nevertheless, in similar vein, Sheila Lawlor of the Centre for Policy Studies has claimed that teacher training 'undermines' the subject specialism of graduates who enter teaching (Lawlor, 1990).

If we were to extrapolate from the case of the school-level reforms (Whitty 1989), we would expect the neo-conservatives among the critics to seek a solution to these problems in rigorous central control of the curriculum of teacher training and entry to teaching. Neo-liberals, on the other hand, might prefer to leave it to employers to decide who is fitted for employment, thus allowing teacher training courses to compete with direct entry routes in the market. And, in broad terms, that distinction does appear to hold up in the literature. However, perhaps to a rather greater degree than was evident in the case of the school reforms, one can also detect an increasing coming together of neo-liberal and neo-conservative solutions. Both views seem to point to the end of the BEd and PGCE as we know them. The neo-conservatives regard most of the existing curriculum of teacher training as dispensable, so in their ideal world the prescribed curriculum would only be a good dose of 'proper subject knowledge'. The neo-liberals would allow schools to go into the market and recruit whomever they wanted, but would expect them in practice to favour straightforward graduates or those with experience in other fields over those who have 'suffered' from teacher training. There is general agreement amongst both groups that, say, two or three years of subject study in a conventional vein is sufficient academic preparation for would-be teachers and any training necessary can be done on an apprenticeship basis in school.

The Thatcher government chose not to apply the National Curriculum to independent schools, and similarly it has not imposed any restrictions (other than those relating to certain criminal convictions) upon those who may be employed as teachers in independent schools and in City Technology Colleges. This suggests that, in situations where market forces already operate more clearly than in the maintained system, government control of teaching qualifications (as of the school curriculum) is seen as unnecessary.

Just as New Right support for a national curriculum is something that may only be needed until a market ideology pervades the system, there is some New Right support for an accreditation body (whether CATE or the proposed Teacher Training Agency) so long as we *do* retain teaching training in anything like the conventional mode. The requirement in Circular 3/84 that student teachers should be taught 'ways in which pupils can be helped to acquire an understanding of a free society and its economic and other foundations' (DES 1984) was an early indication of the re-educative function envisaged for the reformed curriculum of teacher education. Andrew Gamble has suggested that building a strong state through increased expenditure on the apparatuses of law and order, while at the same time using state power to roll back state intervention from other areas of social activity, is not the paradox it at first appears. This is because the state needs to protect the market from being subverted by vested interests (Gamble 1983). One of the reasons why some members of the New Right can believe, at one and the same time, in permitting the entry into teaching of people with little or no training, while imposing increasingly stringent criteria upon the content of established routes into teacher training, lies in its belief that there are 'enemies within'.

At one level this is a general argument about producer interests, but it is also a more specific attack on the alleged ideological bias of teacher educators. Thus a recurring theme in the pamphlets of New

Right pressure groups is the need to rid the system of the liberal or Left educational establishment, which is seen to have been behind the 'progressive collapse' of the English educational system and 'which, prey to ideology and self-interest, is no longer in touch with the public'. It is 'time to set aside...the professional educators and the majority of organised teacher unions...[who] are primarily responsible for the present state of Britain's schools' (Hillgate Group 1987). Particularly worrying to such groups are 'the student radicals of the 1960s, who have marched through to leading positions in departments of education' (Campaign for Real Education 1989). The *Spectator* editorial repeats the usual New Right charge that 'teacher training colleges...are staffed by Marxists who peddle an irrelevant, damaging and outdated ideology of anti-elitism to the trainees in their charge'. It also suggests that removing 'the statutory bar on state schools hiring those with no teacher training qualification...would enable head-teachers to find people...who at the moment are deterred by the prospect of having to waste a year undergoing a period of Marxist indoctrination' (*Spectator*, 27 February 1993, p.5).

So, for the New Right, government control of higher-education-based teacher education courses remains a necessary evil for the time being, but it is not the preferred solution in the long term. Again, the leading article in the *Spectator* has made this explicit:

> Those [teacher training] colleges that survive must be better
> supervised by the Department of Education (sic)....However, if a
> voluntary system of training teachers in schools is allowed,
> within ten years these harmful political training grounds will be
> a thing of the past (27 February 1993, p.5).

But, for the New Right, there was a problem with CATE as a mechanism for 'policing' conventional training courses, in that it seemed to have been taken over by the educational establishment. Even the then Chairman of CATE, Sir William Taylor, was named in the *Daily Telegraph* as an apologist for the educationalists berated in a speech by Prince Charles, while the *Evening Standard* expressed the hope that 'Prince Charles's sterling speech will give the Government confidence to overhaul teacher training colleges root and branch' (23 April 1991). When, despite the antipathy of the educational establish-ment to CATE when it was announced in 1984, one has heard Ted Wragg suggesting that it is a thoroughly modern and appropriate way of safeguarding professional teacher education for the twenty-first century, the New Right's thesis of producer capture gains some credence (BBC Radio 4, 19 February 1991). Yet again, there is a parallel here with the New Right's claim that the educational establishment has hijacked some of the government's National Curriculum working parties. No doubt the proposed Teacher Training Agency is expected to be less susceptible to such influences and, if it is not, the Secretary of State can choose to take his advice from elsewhere.

Government Policy and Teacher Education

Some New Right critics have already called for the end of the BEd and PGCE and for an apprenticeship route to become the major route for teacher training. But, despite the recent threatening developments, this approach has yet to be fully endorsed by the government. To neo-liberal members of the New Right, this is because civil servants, as well as Her Majesty's Inspectorate (HMI), have been incorporated into the producer interests of the educational establishment. Yet, it is perhaps also because the New Right has not entirely thought its position through. In May 1991, *The Times Higher Education Supplement* reported that DES officials had rather unkindly pointed out to government policy advisers keen on reform that it was:

> illogical to assume that people who are the products of 'trendy teacher training of the 1960s'—i.e., today's state schoolteachers—would be best equipped to teach new teachers...this would simply replicate the problem'. (*The Times Higher Education Supplement*, 3 May 1991)

Furthermore, advocates of totally school-based training choose to ignore the fact that, in certain respects, HMI have found the work of experienced teachers no more satisfactory than that of newly-trained ones. It might therefore be argued that, in terms of practical competence (let alone ideological orientation), schools themselves would need to be purged of the 'sixties generation' before they could be trusted by the New Right to carry out teacher training.

Probably far more significant in terms of actual policy-making are the practical problems of handing all initial teacher training over to the schools. Such a shift would involve significant changes in the structure of the teaching profession and the culture of schooling at a time when schools are already having difficulty in coping with existing educational reforms. Only a limited number of schools feel equipped to take on the responsibility, though the financial incentives offered by the latest government initiative may bolster the numbers of those wishing to do so (Pyke 1993). There is even some evidence from recent discussions with secondary headteachers that a few may use this opportunity to help resolve cash crises in schools, suggesting that the apparent tension between training teachers and educating children (HMI 1991) may be removed by an imperative to train teachers for cash in order to maintain the education of children. However, recent surveys by the Standing Conference of Principals and the National Association of Head Teachers suggest that few primary school heads feel that it would be appropriate or feasible to take on more responsibility for teacher education (*The Times Educational Supplement*, 28 January 1994).

For the time being, then, the vast majority of teachers are continuing to be trained through modified versions of the conventional BEd and PGCE routes, even though higher education institutions are being required to enter into new forms of 'partnership' with schools and increase their proportions of school-based work. The more innovative articled teacher route is to be scaled down, and restricted to primary training, but it still retains a major role for higher education institutions. Even in licensed teacher schemes, LEAs are encouraged (though not required) to involve higher education in their programmes of training, despite the fact that such schemes were partly a response to New Right criticisms of higher education. How far any of this will continue if the Teacher Training Agency is established remains to be seen.

Multiple Routes

Although the four-year BEd (or BA[QTS]) course remains an option within current Circulars, the government has indicated that it expects significant numbers of primary teachers to be trained through three-year undergraduate courses in the future. The case for reducing the four-year course has also been made from within higher education itself. David Hargreaves and his colleagues (Booth et al., 1989) have proposed a course that is effectively three years and one term, while from right at the heart of the teacher training establishment Alec Ross and Sally Tomlinson have floated a proposal for a three-year BEd, with each year lasting forty weeks (Tomlinson and Ross 1991). A few courses of this nature are now being developed. Plans by the Open

University to enter postgraduate initial teacher training, by-passing existing providers, could potentially make more flexible provision available on a national basis. The growth of modularity, credit accumulation and the accreditation of prior learning in the higher education system as a whole will generate a demand for shortened teacher training courses and the recognition of a range of experiences as equivalent to conventional teacher training—and hence worthy of a recognised academic award as well as QTS. Thus, almost independently of the government's policy of encouraging more diverse routes into teaching, demographic trends and service needs are likely to encourage the development of new modes of training and there are good equal opportunities arguments for this.

Our own view is that, in our present state of knowledge, we should neither abandon conventional routes nor oppose the development of alternative ones. However, if we again try to draw parallels from the experience of educational reform in general, it seems likely that multiple routes into teaching (like multiple types of schools—or hospitals—left to compete in the market) will soon arrange themselves into a hierarchy of esteem, particularly if they all have different requirements and lead to different awards. While we do not need homogeneity of provision, we do need a comprehensive structure for teacher education, so that questions of resourcing and quality assurance can be tackled on a coherent and consistent basis. Perhaps one of the few positive things that could be said about the National Curriculum Council's foray into initial teacher training (NCC 1991) is that it tried to identify the common ground between the CATE requirements and the recommendations for licensed teacher training.

Teacher Competences

We now need to develop some clearer criteria for monitoring and comparing training via these various routes. If ways of entering teaching are broadened, then trainees' professional development will have to begin from a variety of baselines. Thus, we will have to tackle the whole question of what Qualified Teacher Status now means. It is in this context that the tentative move that began with Circular 24/89 (DES 1989) towards the specification of exit competences for teacher training courses, rather than merely input, content and process criteria, is of interest. With multiple routes we will need to be mainly concerned with whether teachers have developed appropriate competences, rather than with the nature of the route by which they have achieved them. The notion of a prescribed National Curriculum or core curriculum for teacher training, certainly if specified in terms of the number of hours to be devoted to particular subjects, becomes particularly sterile if applied to people with vastly different back-grounds following vastly different routes to QTS.

While we certainly would not advocate the technicist excesses evident in the USA, or in some FE teacher training here, we do think that the competency approach, particularly if it recognises the importance of underpinning knowledge and understanding and generic professional competences as well as specific classroom skills, is worthy of more exploration than teacher educators sometimes assume (Whitty and Willmott 1991). Even courses based around the concept of the reflective practitioner may not be as incompatible with such an approach as is sometimes suggested. A pamphlet produced by the 'Imaginative Projects' group from Goldsmiths' College, Bristol Polytechnic and Newman and Westhill Colleges, is clearly hostile to the technicist thinking that underlies many com-petence-based approaches, as well as to the ideas of the New Right. But, having told us that 'teaching is not reducible to a set of technical operations nor to the simple transmission of subject knowledge', a defence that the New Right might dismiss as typical of the mystique that surrounds teacher education, it goes on to say they are 'not running away from the issue of the systematic appraisal of teaching competence'. Thus, even the quality of reflectivity can be formulated as a series of competences that can be monitored. Two of the eight examples given are:

- A reflective practitioner can articulate and defend his/her own purpose as a teacher and relate this to other professional opinion;
- A reflective teacher treats teaching as an experimental process, recognising the necessity of turning reflection into action, choosing between alternatives, and critically evaluating the process (Hextall et al., 1991, p.16).

Circular 9/92 made the use of competences mandatory within CATE-accredited courses of secondary initial teacher education, requiring that 'higher education institutions, schools and students should focus on the competences of teaching throughout the whole period of initial teacher training' (DFE 1992). But while providing a largely unob-jectionable (though untheorised) set of competences for courses to work with, Circular 9/92 did not claim to have uttered the final word on competences:

> The statements of competences expected of newly qualified teachers do not purport to provide a complete syllabus for initial teacher training....It is recognised that institutions are developing their own competence-based approaches to the assessment of students (DFE 1992).

This approach is rather surprising in terms of a market model of training for what it offers us is a loose specification of *what* is to be produced through teacher training, while the same circular (and associated CATE guidance) gives a detailed prescription of who is best qualified to be involved in production (teachers) and *where* such people should be sited (schools). What business model is it which first selects the site of production and the personnel and then attends to what should be manufactured?

However, far from demanding further clarification from the government on this matter, it is our view that this lack of specification is to be welcomed since it provides us with some space to think about what kind of teaching we want to shape and encourage. It is therefore crucial to use the space provided by Circular 9/92 wisely. In addition, allowing individual institutions and their partner schools the opportunity to experiment with different models may provide the basis for the development of more adequate policy alternatives for the future.

Significantly, the more recent primary Circular, 14/93, does not contain the same implicit invitation for institutions to develop their own approaches to competences. CATE is currently undertaking an exercise to develop the use of teacher competences with beginning teachers and it seems likely that this will form the basis of a national teachers' profile administered through the proposed Teacher Training Agency. In responding to such an exercise, we need to recognise that any account of teaching competences has implicit within it a view of the relationship between theory and practice and presupposes a particular vision of what is involved in teaching. How these relationships are understood has implications for the nature of and relationship between school- and college-based work and for the details of the organisation of teacher education and professional development.

To illustrate the argument, let us suppose that the following account of what is involved in teaching is one on which we can agree:

> Teaching is a complex and dynamic process which involves

exploration, choice, decisions, creative thinking and the making of value judgements (Hextall et al. 1991).

It follows from this account that each piece of teaching is theory-laden. When we watch someone teach, we are not just concerned about their observable behaviour. They have made decisions, they have intentions and purposes, they have made assumptions about the learning process and about learners. Each instance of teaching is at one and the same time theory *and* practice, and they are inseparable. It may be possible to replace some theoretical perspectives with others, but we cannot rid practice of theory. For example, we could replace 'namby-pamby utopianism, naive egalitarianism and the 1960s culture of anything goes' (Marsland 1992) with 'macho realism, sophisticated elitism and the 1990s culture of nothing goes'. But we would be replacing theory with theory, not theory with nothing and, if theory and practice are inseparable, then it follows that both must be the concern of the school and the higher education institution.

Any account of competences must express both the complexity of teaching in general and the relationship between theory and practice in particular. This point becomes particularly obvious in considering the issue of assessment. In assessing competence, we need access not only to what students do but how and why they choose some courses of action rather than others. A simple checklist of typical classroom-based teacher behaviours will not provide an adequate account of competence, because it fails to give us access to that 'why' question that is the mark of the informed professional. In constructing statements of competence which are consistent with our view of what is involved in teaching, we *must* give due weight to the knowledge and understanding which inform practice and to the students' capacity to engage in critical self-evaluation. While this point is hardly new (Wolf 1989; McElvogue and Salters 1992), the work which remains to be done is to find a language which expresses competence in non-dualistic terms. This poses a considerable challenge when the knowledge and understanding integral to teacher action is being used to inform our judgement that someone is a competent teacher as well as a teacher competent in a particular context.

Partnership in Teacher Education

If the use of competences involves unpacking or making explicit what an account of good practice is in a way which does not separate theory from practice but approaches the activity in a holistic way, then there are important implications for the process of teacher education. Observation of experienced teachers in their classrooms is clearly important here, but it will not give students access to the knowledge and understanding which informs the practice of experienced teachers. Therefore, teachers working with students need time to make the bases of their judgements explicit and open to discussion. In other words, they need time to discuss their practice and, at least initially, they may well need support in learning or remembering how to make their decisions and judgements explicit. Evidence is already emerging from the experience of new partnership arrangements which suggests that experienced teachers feel that they have developed competence in some respects and lost it in others. Under the pressure of a welter of changes introduced at breathtaking speed, some teachers have claimed that their 'reflective competence' has drained away.

Students also need to spend time away from the context of any particular school for a variety of alternative perspectives and strategies to be shared and examined. There needs to be time too for them to experience a variety of resources, not all of which will be available within any one school. This may include anything from say, a variety of computer facilities through to actual teaching styles. As one student said in her end-of-term review of her developing competences:

> I wouldn't have really understood what the teacher was doing
> when she set the class to work in groups unless I'd experienced
> this way of working myself in college, and had the chance to
> talk about it as a teaching strategy.

At least until there is a better alternative, higher education institutions provide an important context for time away from the particular school for a variety of purposes, practical as well as theoretical. It would seem to be an act of wanton destruction to dismantle the sites that are already providing for and resourced to fulfil this vital function.

It is, of course, less time consuming, and therefore less expensive in the short term, to concentrate on whether one can perform in a certain way rather than on whether that performance is appropriate. But, in the longer term, it can surely not be the best way to produce effective professional teachers. Furthermore, the notion that critical reflection on one's own practice has to wait until one has been socialised into existing work practices is both intellectually unconvincing and belied by the evidence of the best practice within ITT at the present time.

The 'teacher as researcher' elements of some BEd degrees could well serve as a model for developing reflective qualities in all learner teachers. Such courses have often helped students to develop reflective skills that are not evident in all serving teachers nor, indeed, part of the culture of all schools. The evidence from long-standing studies about professional socialisation, and from some more recent work in New Zealand (Munro 1989), is that beginning teachers are likely to continue to develop such skills only if they are actively encouraged to integrate practice with theory (and vice versa) and if they have on-going support in doing so. Given the variable disposition of skills in different parts of the system at the present time, this is most likely to happen through a genuine partnership between schools, LEAs and higher education institutions.

Even so, there is a danger that the rhetoric of 'partnership' and 'reflective practice' will be used to pave the way for a New Right model of teacher education. In developing competence-based approaches to teacher education with our partner schools, we are perhaps creating the conditions for a more radical move to school-based training in advance of proper dialogue or discussion about the ways in which this might be desirable and for whom. It is also possible that by concentrating on 'reflective practice' as a means of opposing mechanistic models of teaching, we inadvertently collude with an individualised account of the professional teacher as someone who earnestly strives to perfect his or her own practice at the cost of understanding teaching as a social activity. The consequence of this could be to inhibit the perception of issues in teaching as social ones requiring collective, rather than merely individual, action.

All this may sound like a typical example of self-interested higher education-based teacher educators defending their own role and peddling an outmoded perspective in the face of New Right demands for teacher training to be transferred entirely to the schools. However, we would not necessarily want to claim that the present form and balance of higher education involvement in teacher education is correct or that there is a simple formula that applies in all cases for all time. Indeed, multiple routes will produce multiple solutions. But, in the light of what is happening in the USA, we do need to be extremely cautious about any routes that involve no higher education involvement or even those that treat higher education as a sub-contractor for particular purposes in the manner envisaged by David Hargreaves (1990).

First, there is some evidence that the mentor system as practised in California, for example, is a poor vehicle (and certainly an inconsistent one) for sensitising trainee teachers to equal opportunities issues. If higher education is involved just in training mentors and fails to provide a continuing support network, this tendency is exacerbated. For the New Right, this might be an argument in favour of pursuing the mentor system, though it can be countered by asking how we can possibly enhance quality and improve achievement in schools (let alone respond to the current moral panic about youth behaviour) without addressing the needs of all children. Second, in some of the schemes, particularly the famous New Jersey one favoured by the New Right and visited by our HMI (HMI 1989), the involvement of higher education staff in training new teachers does not necessarily disappear—but it takes place on a contractual basis rather than a committed one. However, rather than this market relationship necessarily leading to an improvement in the quality of what higher education offers, as seems to be implied by Hargreaves (1990), its contribution can become even more detached from the reality of teaching because people are brought in to do a discrete job (for example, an updating course during the vacation) with absolutely no knowledge of or sensitivity to the trainees' ongoing work situation.

There are, however, some positive lessons to be derived from the US experience. Professional Development Schools, as advocated by the Holmes Group in the USA (Holmes Group 1990), are one interesting development. These are a variant of the teaching schools idea, involving a partnership between higher education, schools and school districts. School-based training of the licensed teacher variety, geared primarily towards solving teacher supply rather than teacher quality issues, could lead to trainees being inducted largely in poor schools—creating poor quality teachers and probably a high drop-out rate into the bargain. The HMI report on the licensed teacher scheme showed that 'many of those licensed teachers who were performing poorly were in schools which were considered unsatisfactory for the training of teachers' (OFSTED 1993). On the other hand, there is a danger in the teaching school idea that one creates elite schools which bear little relationship to the reality of the mass of schools in which trainees will eventually teach. A consortium approach involving LEAs, schools and higher education institutions allows one to plan for and support a range of experience for all trainees, potentially retaining some role in teacher training for *all* schools and hence a link which, when properly managed, can contribute to the professional development of schools as well as of the trainees. However, on top of this, there may be a case for a few Professional Development Schools, linked to LEAs, higher education institutions and a network of other schools, offering facilities for specialist aspects of initial training, further professional development and research. In some areas, this might provide a new role for (re)integrated City Technology Colleges, which would enable the disproportionate investment in them to be put to the benefit of the service as a whole.

A Common Framework for Teacher Education

It may then still be possible to conceive of an alternative approach to the reform of teacher education to the one prescribed by the New Right—an alternative that recognises that some of the criticisms are justified, that new approaches are called for, but also that there is a lot of good practice and innovation going on within conventional routes (and not just at Oxford and Sussex Universities) and that those routes do still serve important needs. Above all, we urgently need a framework and a set of criteria that will allow us to see all these various developments as part of a coherent system that will ensure some commonality of standards and prevent a diversity of routes into teaching becoming a hierarchy.

This might involve:

- Multiple routes to QTS based on a genuine partnership between training institutions, schools and LEAs.
- Growth in school-based training within this partnership model, but with adequate resources and all trainees treated as supernumerary.
- Recognition of a role in teacher training as part of a teacher's professional responsibilities, together with training for this role.
- Better links between initial training and the first year of teaching, using profiling.
- A coherent approach to ongoing professional development, which provides for continuity and progression between initial training, induction and future staff development and INSET needs.
- A broadly-based, and carefully conceptualised, definition of the competences required by teachers as reflective practitioners.

- The specification of competency criteria that apply to all routes to QTS and the various stages of further professional development.
- Linkage of these competency criteria to a recognised and common structure of awards validated by higher education institutions.
- Monitoring of academic validation through a quality assurance system, based on the best practice developed under the Council for National Academic Awards (CNAA).
- Administration of professional accreditation through a reconstituted and representative version of CATE or through a General Teaching Council (GTC), with strong extra-professional representation to ensure public accountability.
- Sensitivity to local and sectional needs within this national framework.

But it is far from clear how we might now reach a position where anything as coherent as this could emerge from the present atmosphere of confusion and suspicion. As we have seen, the changes in teacher education are part of a much broader change in the nature of education policy-making. The Thatcher government presided over a sharp shift away from the pressure group or quasi-corporatist mode of policy-making that had dominated the era of social democratic consensus from the 1940s to the 1970s—when national government, local education authorities and the organised teaching profession were widely regarded as 'partners' in the education policy-making process. Whether or not this partnership was ever quite what it appeared, it has now been replaced by what one commentator has termed 'an unreconciled and inchoate mixture of central government and a newly enfranchised, dispersed, pluralist array of decision-makers' (Raab quoted in Whitty 1990). In mounting its attack on teacher educators, the government has similarly bypassed the traditional routes of education policy-making, since it regards teacher training institutions, like LEAs, as amongst the foremost examples of 'producer capture' by the liberal educational establishment.

Yet the defence of teacher education is too often still being conducted within the assumptions of the 'old' politics of education with insufficient recognition of the extent to which the world has changed. The assumption still seems to be that meetings between university academics, teacher union officials, local authority directors, inspectors and permanent officials from the Department for Education can set the agenda for the future of teacher education. Parents, teachers, students, industrialists and even politicians remain marginalised in our strategies. It is therefore easy for the government to characterise us all as self-serving members of the 'swollen state'.

So what strategic lessons might we learn from this? First, the New Right seeks to influence politicians rather than bureaucrats. Second, government seeks support for its policies from the public rather than from the professions. Insofar as it does seek the support of professionals, it does so directly rather than through their trade unions or representative bodies. The government's rhetoric is about giving control of teacher education to teachers in schools, rather than to the teaching profession as a collectivity through a General Teaching Council. As with its broader policies of 'devolution', the government has thus been able to characterise itself as democratic and the educational establishment as elitist. It has managed to achieve this even while, in reality, it has also been increasing the powers held at the centre. Furthermore, it has sought to contrast our backroom politics with its own legitimacy via the ballot box and compare our restrictive and monopolistic practices unfavourably with its own apparent commitment to the free market.

In 1992, teacher educators 'celebrated' a minor victory for traditional pressure-group politics, the government's consultation exercise on the Clarke proposals having led to a 'retreat' from the idea of making 80 per cent of PGCE secondary courses school-based. However, probably far more significant in the modification of the proposals than our own arguments or our lobbying of permanent officials were the change of government ministers and the practical problems of handing initial teacher training over to the schools to a tight timetable. It now appears that the government's retreat was a largely tactical one in preparation for the more wide-ranging reforms, more in line with the ideas of Sheila Lawlor and other fanatics of the New Right, and subsequently contained in the 1993 Education Bill.

Before those proposals gain further momentum, teacher educators clearly need to find ways of speaking meaningfully both to the political wing of government and to those 'new' constituencies to whom government chooses to appeal—and not just to those with whom we have traditionally done business behind closed doors. We need to defend only the defensible and develop a form of teacher professionalism which is consistent with legitimate demands for democratic accountability. It is a sad comment on the current state of educational politics that the only apparent hope of limiting the effects of the government's current attack on teacher education and of defending the positive features of teacher professionalism lies with the constitutional anachronism of an unelected House of Lords.

PART 3
CONTROL

7 ALTERNATIVE EDUCATION POLICIES: SCHOOL INSPECTION

Eric Bolton

The progressive involvement of central government in the school curriculum and its assessment, through the 1970s and 1980s, began to make it clear that, regardless of which party was in power, central government would play a more direct role in what went on in schools in relation to curricular content, standards and relevance, while giving more freedom in the day-to-day decision-making to individual schools.

There are some important differences of emphasis between the parties in this respect, but it is highly unlikely that a Labour or Liberal Democratic government would step back from the kind of freedom given to schools under the Local Management of Schools (LMS) regulations, or that they would not have some kind of national curriculum. It seems equally likely that, given the common ground between the political parties, none of them, in government, would drop the intention of better informing parents about the performance of schools, and of their children within them. Once again, there are differences of emphasis, but the main parties' election manifestos at the last General Election made it clear that some kind of regular inspection of schools would take place, and that schools and parents would have access to the findings of those inspections.

That being so, it is not surprising that in the run-up to the Education Reform Act (ERA), Kenneth Baker pronounced that he intended to establish a national curriculum and its associated assessment for all pupils of compulsory school age, and to push decision-making in education to 'the rim of the wheel'. When that phrase was first used by Kenneth Baker to the local education authority national representatives, they thought he meant that decision-making would increasingly rest with them at the local level. It soon became clear, however, that the rim of the wheel, in the then government's eyes, lay much further out from the centre than did the LEAs. Essentially the rim was at the level of individual schools.

It has often been claimed by political and education commentators that the ERA is a mess because it does not seem to know whether it is centralising, or decentralising legislation. There are intended and unintended confusions and tensions in the ERA. Some of those concern centralisation and decentralisation. However, the establishment of more central direction for the curriculum, and its associated assessment, were seen, deliberately and consciously by the then government, as prerequisites for justifying and enabling much more decision-making to be made at the individual school level. To put it bluntly, the government saw itself fulfilling its duties under education law by insisting on a national curriculum for all pupils that would not take up all the time available, and in building in the associated regulations for assessment and reporting.

Those being in place, the government could then claim that all schools were required to satisfy curricular law, and would be called to account in respect of it via national assessment and public reporting. Beyond that, the schools were free to organise things as they wished, and to do whatever else they wanted to do in ways that best suited them. In other words, to justify pushing many decisions out to the rim of the wheel, education law had to insist that all schools do 'X' and be called to account in respect of it.

That kind of policy thinking quickly raised the issue of wider accountability. Clearly the national curriculum, its assessments, and the public reporting of the outcomes of those assessments, would form an important set of checks and balances on the system. However, the government was clear that the best check-and-balance system of all was that of informed parents and local communities who, on a daily basis, would be in touch with what was going on, and be sufficiently well-informed to enter into a constructive dialogue with teachers about their children's education, or the role of the school in the local community. A particular issue, therefore, became that of school inspection. The specific challenge was to establish arrangements whereby each and every school would be inspected and publicly reported upon sufficiently regularly and frequently to enable all parents to have access to up-to-date inspection reports about their children's schools.

There were only four possibilities. The first was to greatly expand Her Majesty's Inspectorate (HMI) from its number of around 450 to something just over 2000. The second was to influence the LEA Inspectorate and Advisory Service's *modus operandi*. The third was to adopt a system rather like that of the French Académie, namely to create a small, influential, national inspectorate with a larger, linked regional inspectorate. The fourth was to put inspection into a more-or-less open market in which demand would generate the inspectors required.

There were a number of reasons why the increase in HMI was a non-starter. Quite apart from the fact that the Conservative government and some of its supporters have never wholly trusted HMI, the costs of increasing the national inspectorate on such a scale were prohibitive. In addition, the collective judgement that was the great strength of HMI would probably not survive such an increase in size. In addition, the conditions of service of a national inspectorate would be unlikely to attract enough people of sufficiently high calibre.

In many ways, given the history of public education in England and Wales, the most sensible solution would have been for the LEA Inspectorates and Advisory Services to be geared up to carry out regular and frequent inspection of schools. After all, at the time, the schools belonged to the LEAs, and the majority still do, and that is where the immediate responsibility for them lies. In addition, the LEA Inspectorates were a ready-made body of some 2000 plus men and women able to adapt to the new needs for inspection.

Unfortunately, inspection practice at the local authority level was extremely uneven, and in some places neither wholly respectable, nor respected. Some local education authorities had always ruled out inspection. Others had carried out inspections of various kinds. None, in any regular way, had published reports locally of the findings of those inspections.

Furthermore, there were some serious doubts about LEA Inspectorates and Advisory Services taking on the new role. Those were of two types. The first and most chronically difficult problem arose from the fact that, for good and proper reasons, many LEAs appointed advisory teams to promote and further particular approaches to teaching and learning. Those may have been subject specific, as was the case with Nuffield science, or phase specific, as in certain approaches to primary organisation and teaching. The practice of using advisory teams, while generating some influential and positive developments in schools over the years, was somewhat counter-productive when seeking to justify a case for those same people to carry out no-axe-to-grind inspections of schools, and to report as they found.

The second issue also concerned the objectivity of local advisory services and inspectorates. That concern was fuelled by the practices of a small number of LEAs in which there was circumstantial evidence of political interference in education locally. The government's deep-rooted suspicion was that many, if not all, Labour-run authorities were seeking to influence politically what went on in their schools, in part through the work of local inspectors and advisers. For those reasons any hope that a Conservative government led by Mrs Thatcher would enhance the role of LEA inspectorates was simply a non-starter.

The French model was toyed with for a time, but it was never a strong runner. It would involve a large increase in the number of civil servants, as that is what regional inspections entail; it would have an immediate and visible impact on public expenditure; it was altogether too French in its mandarin/bureaucratic style, and it left HMI intact, and even more influential.

The fourth possibility was to put inspection in the marketplace by creating a requirement in law for all schools to be inspected and reported upon regularly and frequently; giving schools the money that had to be spent on such inspection, and letting the market take care of meeting the demand. Of course, there would be some regulatory structure around both the inspections themselves, and their reporting, and about the people who would be allowed to inspect. Essentially, however, with local authority inspectorates being prevented from inspecting and reporting on schools in their areas, and by insisting in law that every school be inspected on a regular and frequent basis, and that the reports be published, a market for inspection would be created.

Given the macro-philosophy of the Conservative government, the public expenditure and bureaucratic implications of doing the task any other way, and the government's antipathy towards LEAs, there was never really any doubt about which of the alternatives would be chosen.

The preference for the market solution was further accentuated when, under Mr Major as prime minister, the Citizens' Charter emerged as his distinctive domestic policy line, prior to the last General Election. Within that, the notion of promising every parent that there would be an inspection report available to them during their children's period in school, along with the populist appeal of dressing it up as breaking the 'control of the education establishment', proved irresistible. The idea for what was to become the Office of Standards in Education (OFSTED) was hatched (Bates 1991).

This is not the place to go into detail about OFSTED. Its remit and *modus operandi* have been well publicised. Suffice it to say, that OFSTED was established constitutionally as an independent office of government. Its duties are to organise, plan and oversee the regular, frequent inspection of schools: inspection that, essentially, will be carried out by others. The current remit of OFSTED was much influenced by two amendments to the legislation in the House of Lords. The amendments were accepted by the then government because of the proximity of the General Election. To have tried to upset them would have risked the whole legislation falling. The effect of those amendments was to prevent schools from choosing their own inspectors, to put OFSTED in charge of the contracting for inspection, and to make it the holder of the money for inspection.

Quite apart from anything else those amendments may have achieved, they added a substantial administrative, not to say bureaucratic, burden to OFSTED. There have been signs that some of those advising the present government still hanker after a more market-led solution to school inspection. They are seeking to re-open the debate, and to rescind the House of Lords amendments. Their stated reasons are that what is perceived as the 'education establishment' has retained control of inspection, in that most of the professional staff of OFSTED are HMI; and that a large proportion of the new Registered Inspectors are either ex-HMI, or ex-LEA inspectors, or advisers (Lawlor, 1993).

OFSTED works to a framework-for-inspection that guides the practice of inspections, and what is to be reported on. The inspectors, in part at least, inspect according to predetermined standards, in that the performance of the schools is judged in respect of the standards expected and set out within the National Curriculum. Furthermore, OFSTED is now described as being wholly independent of government. That means that it is now a separate entity divorced from working directly within the DFE, and, in principle, free to publish as it wishes.

Its task is clearly outward looking, in that its main thrust is to ensure regular and frequent inspection of schools. It will report to the schools themselves, and to their governing bodies and parents. The plan is that inspectors will essentially report on how schools are doing and tell them what they need to do to improve. In respect of broader messages about the state of the education service, for society at large, and for the government, the position is less clear. It is intended that some of those important general messages will be extrapolated from the body of institutional inspection. In addition the Secretary of State will be able to ask OFSTED to report to him or her about specific matters.

The success of the project arrangements for carrying out regular and frequent inspection of schools will largely depend upon whether the human and material resources available are sufficient, and, most importantly, whether the arrangements in place can actually withstand the mass of paper that will be generated by the inspections, and by the bureaucratic processes of contracting and paying for them.

The least satisfactory aspect of OFSTED's task is that of providing, in future, inspection-based judgement and advice about the state of the education service nationally that will influence and inform policy development, and be available when it is necessary, whether or not it is asked for by ministers. That task, for the previous 150 years, was the prime duty of HMI.

HMI was never a control inspectorate, inspecting to enforce regulations, nor a standards inspectorate in the sense of inspecting wholly in order to report against predetermined, externally set standards. The nearest HMI came to that was during the period of payment by results. However, even then, while visiting every school to hear children read in order to determine the payment of grant, HMI was inspecting more generally and reporting more widely. That was evident, particularly in the reports and writings of one of the most famous of Her Majesty's Inspectors, Matthew Arnold. In fact, it was reports of those like Arnold, about the damaging consequences of payment by results, that contributed to its demise.

From its beginnings, the duties of HMI remained much the same. In general terms it was to report to the government on the state of the education service and the standards being achieved, and on whether or not the nation was getting value for money. The main tasks of HMI were restated in modern terms, in the Scrutiny of the Inspectorate carried out under the auspices of Lord Rayner's office in 1981. Those duties were, first to provide the government of the day with the information, advice and judgement needed to inform its policies for education; second, to inform of the findings of its inspections those with a direct responsibility for providing or carrying out education; third, and rather quaintly worded, 'to spread good as it goes'.

Never at any point in its history was HMI wholly, or constitutionally, independent of government. All HM Inspectors were civil servants, and the independence of the inspectorate was essentially an independence of professional judgement. The visible and outward signs of that independence of professional judgement were that, while the inspectorate was not free to publish at will (in fact, publication of its findings was always to be determined by the government), if its findings were to be published, they had to be published as they were written by HMI. Neither ministers, nor civil servants could ask for them to be changed. Second, the Head of the Inspectorate, the Senior Chief Inspector, had direct access to the Secretary of State, and did not have to deal with ministers via the Permanent Secretary, or other civil servants. Third, the inspectorate, while having to respond to requests for advice and information from ministers, itself decided how best to gather that information, and on what to base its advice. Fourth, and finally, the inspectorate managed itself and carried out its own appointments, under the aegis of the Civil Service Commissioners.

Thus, throughout its existence, HMI has had to work out, and renegotiate the detailed nature of its independence of judgement, and of its public profile. That is in part because the nature of government interest changes over time and because, while HMI's inspection findings must be professionally determined, it had to gauge how deeply it could, or should, become involved in translating that professional advice into policy and practice through its relationship with departmental officials and ministers.

Consequently, despite changes over time, some things about HMI remained the same. The first was that, to gauge the main concerns of the inspectorate at any given time, one needed to look to what the government's interest in education was. Putting it crudely, when governments were much involved and interested in education, such as now, HMI had a high profile and would be inspecting and reporting in relation to policy, either to advise about the development of policy, or to report on how it was developing in practice. When government interest was limited, as in the 1960s, HMI was much less publicly visible and the reports were few.

Whether or not reports saw the light of day depended upon the government and its education ministers. However, the reality was that when education had a high political profile, and the work of HMI was very visible, it proved difficult for governments to withhold publication of the findings of inspection.

In the early 1980s Education Minister Sir Keith Joseph determined that all HMI institutional inspection reports should be published as a matter of course. Speaking then, he described them as the most important change-agent in education. That decision, about institutional inspection reports, started an unstoppable process in which the reports of all HMI inspections and surveys were published routinely. Some 11 years or so later, another Conservative Secretary of State, Kenneth Clarke, was to take a very different line about the publication of HMI reports. He found it counter-productive to have a body like the national inspectorate, as he described it, going round the country reporting publicly on the government's policies in practice, warts and all. No doubt the rather different lines taken by those two Tory education ministers had more than a little to do with the fact that Keith Joseph was looking at an education scene in which his political opponents had been active, as the government, for some years. On the other hand, Kenneth Clarke was looking back over a period of some 12 years of Conservative governments, all of which had been highly active in education. In those circumstances, it is perhaps understandable that the inspectorate came to be seen as made up of troublesome priests, rather more than of constructive change-agents.

The Conservative government was right in judging that there was a need for a system of regular and frequent institutional inspections of schools, and that the reports of those inspections should be published. HMI could not be the body to do that, without changing beyond recognition. Whether or not the chosen solution will work remains to be seen. There must be serious doubts, largely over whether or not OFSTED will develop, within its scattered and variable field force, the sound collective judgement that will generate the respect it will need to be influential in the land. A further doubt centres on OFSTED's capacity to survive the immensely bureaucratic and paper-driven exercise on which it seems to be embarking (OFSTED 1993). Leaving those concerns aside, the main contention of this paper is that the nationally important inspection and advisory functions that were carried out by HMI are at risk, if not already mortally wounded.

HMI's task was to report on the state of the education service nationally, on the basis of wide-ranging inspection of what actually went on *in situ*. It had to report to the government, in the first instance, and had to play some part in translating that professional advice, should it be taken, into practice. In other words, at its best, the national inspectorate was able to provide an inspection-based, professional input to the policy-making and executive arms of government. That could, and did, ensure on many occasions that government policies were professionally sure-footed. That is not to say that they were always the best policies for education, nor indeed that they were uncontentious. A clear example of that professional input to policy is the work of HMI on the curriculum over the past 20 years or so.

It is difficult to see how that particular role is to be carried out, with any certainty, within the new arrangements for inspection. Given its remit, HMI had to report, and be in a position to report, on issues as they were becoming of policy interest, as well as on policy implementation. To do that, particularly if the issues had large-scale implications, required extensive inspection based on some kind of national sample. It is pointless to start such a programme of inspection when the government actually needs inspection-based information and advice. Indeed, large-scale, national inspections may take three or four years from the planning stage to the final report.

The extent to which, over the years, HMI was able to carry out the 'right' inspections, and to report in a timely fashion, was dependent upon the national inspectorate being within, but not wholly of, national policy and executive arrangements.

The business of inspection and advice is a two-way conduit: advice from inspection needs to feed back through the system to those with executive and legislative responsibilities, but for inspection to be focused and timely, data and judgement about what will be required, and when, must feed through that conduit and percolate out to inspectors in the field, and influence their work and priorities. Crucial to the effectiveness of that two-way process was the fact that, within the old HMI set-up, the Senior Chief Inspector was also a Deputy Secretary within the DES. That meant that the SCI was one of only four deputy secretaries responsible for all the policy branches in the DES. In addition, and along with the Permanent Secretary, those four deputy secretaries were the most senior officials in the Department. That meant that the SCI was involved in, and/or present at, the most senior discussions of policy and priorities, including residential sessions with ministers when they reviewed future needs in the light of their policy.

That level of involvement enabled the SCI to feed into the senior planning group of the inspectorate guidance about the priorities for inspection that would be needed to ensure that the inspectorate would be in a position to provide appropriately focused, timely, inspection-based evidence and advice. The involvement of the SCI at the top of the Department and the inspectorate was replicated at the level of the chief inspectors and the heads of DES policy branches; and of staff inspectors and the heads of particular programmes within those branches, and more widely with the world of education outside, particularly in crucial quangos covering curriculum, examinations, assessment and teacher training.

It was also crucial that HMI independence had to be worked out in the difficult yet fruitful context of being in, but not wholly of, the government machine. Determining anew the parameters of that independence in changing political and professional circumstances, enhanced the influence of HMI. In part that was because everyone knew that HMI was charged with reporting as it found, but also because it had to negotiate and argue through its findings with those at the most senior levels of education policy formulation and implementation. In addition, having constantly in mind the need to give useful advice and judgement, and to help, professionally, in translating some of this into practice, kept HMI's collective feet on the ground.

One of the great risks of a wholly independent professional advisory body, without executive powers, like HMI, is that it loses contact with *realpolitik*, and the class and lecture rooms in which teachers work. That can cause it to become an irresponsible, kite-flying body, airing its own particular whims and prejudices. While that accusation might be levelled at some individual HMI judgements over the years, it was never true of HMI's collective judgement and advice on major issues.

That is not to say that HMI was always right, far from it. But it is the case that what it said collectively was based on what was actually going on, and its judgements were reasonable extrapolations from that reality, influenced by its professional expertise and knowledge. HMI was that kind of inspectorate: it had no magic wands; no blueprints for education, and no axes to grind. It derived its advice from inspection carried out by itself. It consisted of a collection of individuals, each of whom was an experienced and successful educationalist in his or her own right, with standing and integrity in the fields in which he or she operated. Working together those individuals described good practice as they found it, and pointed out to those with executive powers what needed to be addressed if it were to be more widely spread. They also drew attention to shortcomings and to what was needed to bring about improvements.

HMI asked that what it had to say be seriously considered, but it was for others to decide what was to be done, be those others national or local politicians, administrators, heads or teachers. How close or distant HMI should be in relation to government and civil servants was a matter of specific judgement case by case. People outside the inspectorate were more inclined to believe in the independence of HMI when it seemed to be critical of government policy than when what it had to say seemed to support it. That is understandable, but the fact is that for HMI's findings to support or criticise government policy was simply something that happened as a consequence of those findings. It was not something determined in advance by any particular stance of the inspectorate, nor was it attributable to coat-trailing a particular line on education.

Given that complex reality, in particular the inward-looking and subtle relationship between a body of professionally independent advisers, and the executive and legislative arm of government, it is interesting to examine the particular constitutional arrangements made for OFSTED, and the particular direction in which its remit points. The government insists that it has made OFSTED completely independent. It has done so by creating a constitutional position for the Office of Inspection and HM Chief Inspector.

It might be no more than an echo of Greeks bearing gifts, but when a government, particularly a government as deeply and specifically involved in changing education policy and practice as this one is, gives a national inspection body, charged with reporting what is going on, complete independence, it is not surprising that there is an uncomfortable pricking of thumbs. Complete independence in important matters is an indication of complete irrelevance. There might well be something of that in the situation we now face. By removing OFSTED and setting it up physically at some distance from the DFE, and disentangling it from that difficult and complex inter-relationship experienced by HMI, the government has removed most of the ways in which a national inspectorate can keep abreast of policy. It has also made more formal, distant and difficult the inspectorate's opportunities constantly to feed professional thinking into policy formulation and implementation.

The rhetoric about complete independence, and disentangling the inspectorate from ministers and civil servants has a populist and simple appeal: it seems on the side of the angels. That is profoundly misleading, and it is likely the new arrangements will turn out to be damaging to education. Institutional inspection, conducted as a programme determined solely by a requirement for frequent and regular inspection of all schools, will not lead to sharply focused and timely inspection reports about the state of the education service nationally, and many of the particular elements that were typical of HMI at its best, will be lost. Nor will an inspection programme of that kind allow a continuation of that reporting about policy implementation that has characterised the last 10 or 15 years. The capacity of OFSTED to conduct that kind of inspection programme nationally, regularly and frequently is at best seriously impaired, or at worst non-existent.

Furthermore, the remaining HM inspectors within OFSTED will not themselves be the main agents of inspection. Consequently, to the extent that they do comment nationally about the state of the education service, they will be doing so not on evidence gathered by them, but on the findings of inspection carried out by others, and a somewhat variable crew of others at that. Therefore, whether or not the new national inspection arrangements competently and effectively deliver a programme of regular and frequent institutional inspection, the kind of work carried out over the years by HMI in reporting about the service nationally will largely disappear from the scene. Institutional inspection's findings will not suffice as a basis for any systematic checks or balances on ministers and policy-makers when formulating and drafting policy, nor will they feed in information and advice, in a sufficiently focused and timely fashion, to policy implementation. For example, if, as is likely, the English tests presently formulated for Key Stage 3 go ahead, who will report, authoritatively, on the consequences of that implementation? How will any one, government, educators, employers, parents, or society at large, have access, in future, to a more-or-less independent, no-axe-to-grind, professional comment on what is actually taking place? There does not appear to be any way in which that kind of inspection can take place on any regular basis in the future. Trying to draw that kind of advice out of general, institutional inspection is far too vague and diffuse and is unlikely to be achievable in the time-scale that politics and action in the real world demand.

In relation to inspection and advice, something of value is in the process of being discarded without having been discussed seriously. Most of the debate about the new inspection arrangements, in all political parties, and within education, has concentrated on the questions of school inspection, privatised inspectors, lay inspectors, and on a simplistic notion of independence. Partly because of the complexity, subtlety and inward-looking nature of the long and difficult relationship between civil servants, government and HMI, merits and shortcomings were never discussed. Yet it was that relationship, its difficulties and complexity, allied with the professionalism of HMI, that contributed crucially to the influence, effectiveness and usefulness of national inspection. There is a serious risk that that will be lost in the new arrangements. If that does happen it will be damaging to the education service in the longer run.

It need not have happened. The government could have introduced the arrangements it is now establishing for regular and frequent inspection of schools led by registered inspectors but overseen not by OFSTED, but by a national inspectorate of around some 250 HM inspectors. That national inspectorate could have continued to be HMI; to be independent in the way that HMI was independent, and to have worked within the same constructive tension with government and civil servants. At the same time the national inspectorate could have been given oversight of the arrangements for the inspection of individual institutions, and been made responsible for integrating inspection priorities and findings with a programme of policy-driven, national sampling inspection carried out by HMI.

There are too few HM inspectors left in OFSTED for that to happen on any consistent basis. In addition it is likely that they will become increasingly bogged down by the bureaucratic process of organising and overseeing inspection arrangements and the findings of inspections carried out by others.

For 'school inspection' to be effective, influential, and useful, it needs to consist of much more than a programme of institutional inspection carried out in respect of certain externally set standards. If those actively involved in education, civil servants, governments, employers, and society at large, are to have available to them a respected and informed body of information about what is going on, and well-founded judgement and advice about what is needed to bring about improvement and sustain good practice, something like HMI is required. Without that, governments, and everyone else involved, fall prey to whoever shouts loudest, or whoever has access to influential ears.

Over the past decade, international interest in the work of HMI has increased enormously in both developed and third world countries, as governments have come to recognise their need for soundly based information and advice about the public education service. Yet, in Britain, by an act of careless vandalism, driven by ideology and ignorance, we have enacted a small but important tragedy and destroyed it. More important than the end of HMI is the fact that its demise, or its transmogrification into OFSTED, removes from the scene a quiet, authoritative voice that so often spelled out what was really happening in the education service; from time to time stopped foolishness in its tracks; gave some succour to good practice, and by constant drip feed, and occasional deluge, provided a professional input to policy-making and its implementation in education.

8 ALTERNATIVE EDUCATION POLICIES: ASSESSMENT AND TESTING

Paul Black

Back to the Future?

Chesterton said that the trouble with Christianity was not that it had been tried and found wanting but that it had never seriously been tried. I could plead the same for the TGAT recommendations, and have yet another go at bemoaning government's actions. Then this could be a very short piece—the alternative to present policies is *Task Group on Assessment and Testing* (DES 1988a,b).

Lacking the courage to be so arrogant, I shall try instead to go over the ground from the beginning, hoping to bring in some lessons from experience, looking at some of the criticisms of the original proposals and at some of the difficulties that have arisen in practice.

So why do we need assessment at all? The first reason must still be to inform teaching and learning—the formative function. The second and third must be reasons bearing upon the summative function, for the certification of individuals and for accountability. These last two should be kept separate, if only because the accountability function can be satisfied by sampling, which is not possible for the first and second. Overall, assessment is needed for discourse—the dialogue about our aims is made concrete by examples of what it means for pupils to achieve them.

In what follows, I want to look at each of these aims separately. Then I want to look at the interactions, supportive or destructive, which can arise when they have to be combined in a system.

Formative Assessment

The ideal was and is fine. There is ample research evidence that where feedback on performance is used to guide learning, it goes better (see for example Bangert-Drowns et al. 1991, Crooks 1988, Block et al. 1989, Grisay 1991). It is also clear that such assessment has to be developed in accord with four main principles, namely:

☐ formative assessment cannot be stuck on to an existing learning programme, it has to be built in to the design of any programme;

☐ to serve the formative purpose the assessment has to be criterion referenced;

☐ the mere collection of evidence is to no purpose unless it is to be acted upon, so the problems of tuning the teaching to the spread of achievements of pupils in a class have to be addressed;

☐ pupils have to develop their own understanding of what their learning is meant to achieve for them, and to be as clear as possible about their own progress: so, pupils have to be involved in their own assessment.

All of these features bristle with difficulty. There was ample evidence before 1988 that assessment as an integral part of a teaching programme was a concept that was hardly understood at all by the majority of teachers (Black and Dockrell 1982, Black 1986, Hodson 1986). The introduction of national assessment has made very little difference to this situation. Those who have studied teachers' practices and opinions about national assessment frequently find that teachers assume that teacher assessment means summative assessment, so that teachers are trying to replicate the Standard Assessment Tasks (Harlen and Qualter 1991, SEAC 1991a, Bennett et al. 1992, SEAC 1992b). For example, some complain that part of the term at the end of a key stage is wasted because they are 'doing the teacher assessment'. In the case of attainment targets assessed only by teachers' assessment, special set piece occasions are frequently used, again constructing a summative school-made SAT. One study of primary teachers describes three types of response to the needs of national assessment (McCallum et al. 1994). The first is to resist and to adhere to traditional practice. The second is to collect a great deal of evidence, but to make hardly any use of it except to review it at infrequent intervals, so that assessment takes much time and is a burden, with little profit except to satisfy the perceived external demands. The third response is to collect evidence and to review it frequently, so that teaching is attuned to the achievement of pupils.

In various development projects—for example the criterion referencing initiative reported by Black and Dockrell in the mid-1980s (Black and Dockrell 1984), the various Graded Assessment projects (Murphy and Torrance 1988, Ferriman and Lock 1989, Swain 1989)—and some of the progress record schemes introduced by LEAs, teachers have shown the capacity to alter professional practice and come to terms with the introduction of formative assessment. Evaluation reports have shown that it is teachers with this type of experience in their background who have been able to make a constructive response to the national assessment requirements. It can be done, but it takes intensive training, grounded in classroom and curriculum practice in which assessment plays its part. No such programme has been provided on a national scale.

The use of criterion-referenced assessment for formative purposes raises further needs and problems. To be a guide to progress in learning, criteria have to reflect some model of progression. The ten-level system—about the only significant recommendation of TGAT that is still being put into practice—is a response to this need. Some such model is essential, whether it be a national guide or the private construction of each teacher. It is clear that we know far too little about optimising progress in learning to draw up such a model. A patiently researched version, in every area of every subject, is sorely needed (Brown and Denvir 1987, Black and Simon 1992).

Given that this difficulty is, or ought to be, faced by every teacher, it would seem helpful to have a national guideline—but it would have to be one that has been patiently worked out between research and practice. Part of such work should tackle the problem of the degree of specificity needed for useful criterion statements. As in the similar case of the objectives approach to the design of learning, the prospect of death by drowning in a sea of minutiae of qualification is all too apparent—a danger that TGAT tried to avoid but SEAC seemed to want to embrace (Allanson et al. 1990). A specification of domains, and of level-ness within a domain, supported by illustrative examples, is the way to make sense of this. However, this way can only be taken if one accepts that there is no feasible substitute for trusting professional judgement when it comes to a particular piece of work by a particular child.

Going with this is the problem of 'appropriate mastery'. At the moment, SAT assessment has curious rules by which it is decided whether a pupil has attained a level in the light of that pupil's success on the discrete statements of attainment actually tested at that level.

These rules, which have been changed more than once, lead teachers to be very nervous about making similar decisions in respect of their own assessments: they can assess on every statement, but some then want a rule of aggregation. This is not simply a bureaucratic difficulty. The substantive question is—how much does a pupil need to have grasped in order to proceed to the next work rather than go back and repeat the previous work? There cannot be a single answer to this; it will be different between different subjects and even between different aspects of the same subject. Again, as yet we know too little about well-guided progression to give good answers. Of course, if the problem is raised in respect of the summative use of teachers' assessment, the answer will be different—as I shall discuss below.

Summative Assessment for Certification

At issue here are both the high stakes assessments that give pupils school leaving certificates at age 16 and also the assessments which are, or ought to be, passed on with a pupil when (s)he moves from one school to another, and from one year group to the next. This is 'pass-it-on' summative. What is needed therefore is information which is sufficiently detailed to give useful guidance, yet sufficiently parsimonious to be appraised and understood. A uniform scheme of progression criteria is again a very helpful background for this purpose. The struggle to get this function right seems strange—the TGAT idea of profile components was only partially understood, witness the ridiculous hiccups over the large numbers of attainment targets in mathematics and science, subsequently reduced so that the attainment target now has the function that TGAT intended for the profile component.

Two considerations matter here. The first is that the summative function, whether it is carried out by teachers or by external tests or by both, will always threaten the formative function and can derail it entirely. Because of this threat, I believe that teacher assessment must be trusted with at least a part in the summative in addition to its formative function, although the corollary is that teachers will have to struggle with a tension between these two functions of teacher assessment.

The second consideration is that a reliable and valid summative result cannot be achieved by external means which operate in isolation from teachers' assessments. Within any reasonable practical constraints, and given the variability of pupils' performance, over time and over different contexts and types of test demand, external testing cannot achieve either validity or reliability at an acceptable level (Black 1993). Given this, the external must be reduced to being one component, preferably with the function of acting as a calibrating and otherwise informative check on teachers' interpretations and standards. Here there is great scope, for example for the availability of banks of calibrated test items and procedures, broader and more sophisticated in scope than present banks of multiple choice items. The various graded assessment schemes have begun to show the way in this respect.

This leaves the problem of how the two functions of teachers' assessments, the formative and the summative, can be reconciled. Is it enough to say that the summative can simply be the aggregation of the formative? Clearly not, for if progress has been made, the earlier steps are irrelevant at the end. Is it enough to say that the latest, leading edge, of attainment in a scheme of progression is needed? This comes closer, although there are complications because some topics may have been tackled very recently, but not consolidated or used, whilst others may have been directly addressed so long ago that to quote them as present capabilities may seem very uncertain. The State of Queensland in Australia, which has long experience with this issue, uses the phrase 'fullest and latest' to describe their strategy (Butler and Beasley 1987).

Perhaps we worry too much. The traditional test is only a statement that on this date (or dates) some time ago—as far as a user is concerned—this person was able to do these things in the peculiar circumstances of the examination room—one does not have to be too bold to be able to compose a more useful, albeit modest statement. All such statements are valued only for their predictive potential, so the clue might be to ask what aspects of the teachers' knowledge can best be used as predictive guides to the pupil's future. The function of any predictive guide matters here. Possible functions are:

☐ to enable a school to attest that the pupil once achieved knowledge, or understanding, or skill (and so could do it again with preparation);

☐ to attest that the pupil is fluent to this level and able to put into use the knowledge and/or skills at any time;

☐ to predict whether a pupil is capable of carrying on with further study (this is closely related to the formative function);

☐   to proclaim that the pupil did really well and so has special talent in a particular direction.

These, or a mixture of them, could be distilled from a teacher's formative record, supplemented and calibrated perhaps by extra summative exercises; few of them can be distinguished or attested with much confidence from a traditional test. So teachers have to take on a summative role, but in that role they should be using the formative assessment very selectively alongside other information. This needs much development, but we have to be clear that any other solution is fraught with greater difficulties, and even with threats of disaster.

Finally, the aggregation of criteria information is a problem for which the solution may, for summative purposes, be different from that for formative. Given the differences between subjects, it is difficult to generalise. However, for example, in formative use it may be possible to overlook a gap because this can be covered another way later, whilst for summative the gap exists and maybe the later attempt has not succeeded either, so a record of the omission has to be made.

Summative Assessment for Accountability

For overall accountability of the national system, the APU model can work well and it was a pity that it was abandoned. It was patently absurd to imagine that national assessment could fulfil the same function—witness the replacement of Assessment of Performance Unit science, with its 35 hours of separate assessments on a sampling basis as the minimum that research showed was needed to give reliable measures (Black 1990, Johnson 1988), by Key Stage 3 SATs in science of three hours' duration, constrained to yield the separate measures of the levels for each of three ATs.

The accountability need also bears on the confidence that the public has to have about teachers' certification assessments of individuals. TGAT recommended that teachers should have the final say on the level for each individual pupil and that SATs would only determine an overall distribution constraint for each school's results. This idea was very quickly dismissed as either impracticable or undesirable; the Swedes, on the other hand, who have been using it for many years, do not seem to have much difficulty with it (Marklund 1991).

For calibration of teachers' assessments, a bank drawn from APU type survey items and informed by the data from those surveys would serve to strengthen and guide teachers' work. Moderation of school results is also needed to complement use of external calibrated item banks. Here agreement trials on samples of pupils' work have a very important part to play. This again was a central TGAT recommendation that was dismissed—although those researching the implementation of assessment in the National Curriculum have commented on the value for teachers of such procedures where LEAs or school consortia have set them up. Much more of this activity is needed, not merely as a guarantor of uniformity, but as a main channel through which the system does its action research and gives a powerful voice to teachers in improving the assessment system to make it practicable and yet pedagogically effective.

Designing a System

Our present situation is that there is an attempt to serve the Accountability and Certification functions with one set of assessments, whilst the formative function is undervalued, underdeveloped and confused with teachers' summative assessment. In consequence, the curriculum is being driven by the two summative demands. At the same time, and ironically, neither certification nor accountability, let alone the raising of standards, are being well served.

It is possible to have a vision. We can imagine that teachers' formative assessment will one day enrich learning in all classrooms, harnessing pupils' motivation through their understanding of their own learning aims and needs. Then, teachers may also carry out a summative function, using their formative findings, judiciously supported by external assessment resources and peer help through agreement trials. The public will develop confidence in moderated teachers' assessments so that it will be accepted that these assessments give the most reliable and valid information for the certification of pupils' achievements. Finally, a more detailed picture of changes in learning achievements will be provided by detailed tests and assessments conducted through national monitoring on a sampling basis.

All of this is achievable. Much of it is quite close to the best practice that was developing until recently. However, it is all very far from average practice. It will take extensive research and development programmes before the basis of support for teachers is adequate, and a patient programme of teachers' professional development before normal practice can use the opportunities and match the dream. The difficult problem that then remains is to plan an interim period of development.

This has to pay as much regard to present feelings as to logistics and technical efficiency. I can only guess at a good way through. Possible steps would be:

- [ ] a moratorium on all national assessment for four years;

- [ ] phased expansion of the teacher assessment component of 16 + examinations with research into reliability and the effectiveness of moderation methods;

- [ ] the present budget for SATs to be redirected to support groups of schools, selected to work with institutions having research capability on programmes to enhance teacher assessment practices over two years, followed by a two year programme of INSET for all, such programmes to include calibration of teacher assessment through agreement trials and external assessment banks;

- [ ] national assessment then reintroduced at 11 and 14 based on teachers' summative assessment with moderation procedures, perhaps involving external tests as part of the calibration;

- [ ] the question of whether there could be useful national assessment at age 7 to be left until the rest has been re-established, by which time it would be a less highly charged issue than it is at present.

All of this assumes that some related set of initiatives is looking into curriculum reform, and none of it can work well unless that produces outcomes that can harness again the co-operation of most teachers. It will also be essential that curriculum reform produces some clarification about how children are to make progress in their learning and how any national guidelines can be helpful in this regard.

PART 4
CONCLUSION: AN ALTERNATIVE VIEW

9 TOWARDS EDUCATION FOR DEMOCRACY: THE LEARNING SOCIETY

Stewart Ranson

This sketch for a theory of the learning society builds upon the ideas and practice being developed in some parts of Britain. Reforms do not begin *de novo*, they have their origins in local communities which are discovering solutions to dilemmas they confront. Our task is to develop understanding of underlying principles in order to create the basis for the more general application.

Key Components of the Theory of the Learning Society

The theory builds upon three axes: of presupposition, principles and purposes. The *presupposition* establishes an overarching proposition about the need for and purpose of the learning society; the *principles* establish the primary organising characteristics of the theory; while *purposes and conditions* establish the agenda for change that can create the values and conditions for a learning society.

Presupposition

There is a need for the creation of a learning society as the constitutive condition of a new moral and political order. It is only when the values and processes of learning are placed at the centre of the polity that the conditions can be established for all individuals to develop their capacities, and that institutions can respond openly and imaginatively to a period of change. The transformations of the time require a renewed valuing of and commitment to learning—as the boundaries between languages and cultures begin to dissolve, as new skills and knowledge are expected within the world of work and, most significantly, as a new generation rejecting passivity in favour of more

139

active participation requires to be encouraged to exercise such qualities of discourse in the public domain. A learning society, therefore, needs to celebrate the qualities of being open to new ideas, listening to as well as expressing perspectives, reflecting on and enquiring into solutions to new dilemmas, co-operating in the practice of change and critically reviewing it.

Principles

Two organising principles provide the framework for the learning society. The first principle is citizenship which establishes the mode of being in the learning society: the notion of being a citizen ideally expresses our inescapable dual identity as both individual and member of the whole, the public; our duality as autonomous persons who bear responsibilities within the public domain. Citizenship establishes the right to the conditions for self-development but also a responsibility that the emerging powers should serve the wellbeing of the common-wealth. Citizenship I define (cf. Held 1989) as the status of membership of national and local communities which thereby bestows upon all individuals equally reciprocal rights and duties, liberties and constraints, powers and responsibilities. Citizens express the right as well as the obligation to participate in determining the purposes and form of community and thus the conditions of their own association.

The second principle is practical reason, which establishes the epistemology, the mode of knowing and acting of the citizen in the learning society. Practical wisdom describes a number of qualities which enable us to understand the duality of citizenship in the learning society: knowing what is required and how to judge or act in particular situations; knowing which virtues should be called upon. Practical reason, therefore, presents a comprehensive moral capacity because it involves seeing the particular in the light of the universal, and a general understanding of what good is required as well as what proper ends might be pursued in the particular circumstances. Practical reason, thus, involves deliberation, judgement and action: *deliberation* upon experience to develop understanding of the situation, or the other person; *judgement* to determine the appropriate ends and course of action, which presupposes a community based upon sensitivity and tact; and learning through *action* to realise the good in practice.

There is also a necessity to provide the purposes and conditions, new values and conceptions of learning as are valued within the public domain at the level of *the self* (a quest of self-discovery), at the level of *society* (in the learning of mutuality within a moral order), and at the level of the *polity* (in learning the qualities of a participative democracy). These conditions for learning within the self, society and the polity are discussed in turn.

Conditions for a Learning Self

At the centre of educational reforms within the inner city as much as those emerging from the polity itself is a belief in the power of agency: only an active self or public provides the purposes and condition for learning and development. Three conditions are proposed for developing purpose within the self: a sense of agency; a revived conception of discovery through a life perceived as a unity; and an acknowledgement of the self in relation to others.

The Self as Agent

Learning requires individuals to progress from the post-war tradition of passivity, of the self as spectator to the action on a distant stage, to a conception of the self as agent both in personal development and active participation within the public domain. Such a transformation requires a new understanding from self-development for occupation to self-development for autonomy, choice and responsibility across all spheres of experience. The change also presupposes moving from our prevailing preoccupation with cognitive growth to a proper concern for development of the person as a whole—feeling, imagination and practical/social skills as much as the life of the mind. An empowering of the image of the self presupposes unfolding capacities over (a life) time. This implies something deeper than mere 'lifelong education or training'. Rather it suggests an essential belief that an individual is to develop comprehensively throughout his or her lifetime and that this should be accorded value and supported.

The Unity of a Life

We need to recover the Aristotelian conception of what it is to be and to develop as a person over the whole of a life and of a life as it can be led (cf. MacIntyre 1981). This has a number of constituent developments: first, perceiving the life as a whole—the self as developing over

141

a lifetime. Second, therefore, a conception of being as developing over time: life as a quest with learning at the centre of the quest to discover the identity which defines the self. Third, seeing the unity of a life as consisting in the quest for value, each person seeking to reach beyond the self to create something of value, which is valued. Fourth, developing as a person towards the excellences: perfecting a life which is inescapably a struggle, an experience of failure as well as success. Fifth, accepting that the struggle needs to be guided by virtues, which support the development of the self; dispositions which strengthen and uplift character; valued dispositions. Last, acknowledging that the most important virtue is that of deliberation, a life of questioning and enquiry committed to revising both beliefs and action; learning from being a means becomes the end in itself, the defining purpose creatively shaping the whole of a life.

The Self as Persons in Relation

But we can only develop as persons with and through others; the conception of the self presupposes an understanding of how we live a life with each other, of the relationship of the self to others; the conditions in which the self develops and flourishes are social and political. The self can only find its moral identity in and through others and membership of communities. Self-learning needs to be confirmed, given meaning by others, the wider community; what is of value will be contested; therefore we need to agree with others what is to be considered valuable; to deliberate, argue, provide reasons.

The Social Conditions for Learning

The unfolding of the self depends upon developing the necessary social conditions which can provide a sense of purpose within society both for the self and others. These conditions are civitas, active participation in creating the moral and social order, and capacity for interpretive understanding.

Virtues of Civitas: The Civic Virtues of Recognising and Valuing Others, of Friendship

The conditions for the unfolding self are social and political: my space requires your recognition and your capacities demand my support (and vice versa). Jordan (1989) emphasises the importance of mutual responsibility in developing conditions for all individuals to develop their unique qualities. He recalls Aristotle's celebration of civic friendship—of sharing a life in common—as being the only possible route for creating and sustaining life in the city. Such values, arguably, are now only to be found within feminist literature which emphasises an ethic of caring and responsibility in the family and community, and the dissolution of the public as a separate (male) sphere (cf. Gilligan, 1986; Pateman, 1987; Okin, 1991). It is only in the context of such understanding and support that mutual identities can be formed and the distinctive qualities of each person can be nurtured and asserted with confidence.

Creating a Moral Community

The post-war world was silent about the good, holding it to be a matter for private discretion rather than public discourse. But the unfolding of a learning society will depend upon the creation of a more strenuous moral order. The values of learning (understanding) as much as the values which provide the conditions for learning (according dignity and respecting capacity) are actually moral values that express a set of virtues required of the self but also of others in relationship with the self. The values of caring or responsibility upon which can depend the confidence to learn derive any influence they may have from the authority of an underlying moral and social order. The civic virtues, as MacIntyre (1981) analyses, establish standards against which individuals can evaluate their actions (as well as their longer 'quest'); yet particular virtues derive meaning and force from their location within an overall moral framework (what MacIntyre calls a 'tradition'). A moral framework is needed to order relationships because it is the standards accepted by the moral community which provide the values by which each person is enabled to develop.

Yet a moral order is a public creation and requires to be lived and recreated by all members of the community. Each person depends upon the quality of the moral order for the quality of his or her personal development and the vitality of that order depends upon the vitality of the public life of the community. For the Athenian, the virtuous person and the good citizen were the same because the goods which inform a life were public virtues. But the authority of a moral order for the modern world will grow if it is an open morality rather

143

than a socialisation into a tradition. The development of a moral community has to be a creative and collaborative process of agreeing the values of learning which are to guide and sustain life in the community. Simey (1985) and Titmuss (1971) have recorded the emergence of communal virtues which reflect the process of citizens taking ownership and responsibility for their lives.

Interpretive Understanding: Learning to Widen Horizons

Taylor (1985, 1991, 1992) has argued that the forms of knowing and understanding, as much as or at least as part of, a shared moral order, are the necessary basis of civic virtue. Historically conditioned prejudices about capacity, reinforced by institutions of discrimination, set the present context for the learning society. The possibility of mutuality in support of personal development will depend upon generating interpretive understanding, that is on hermeneutic skills which can create the conditions for learning in society: in relationships within the family, the community and at work. In society we are confronted by different perspectives, alternative life-forms and views of the world. The key to the transformation of prejudice lies in what Gadamer (1975) calls 'the dialogic character of understanding': through genuine conversation the participants are led beyond their initial positions, to take account of others, and move towards a richer, more comprehensive view, a 'fusion of horizons', a shared understanding of what is true or valid. Conversation lies at the heart of learning: learners are listeners as well as speakers.

The presupposition of such agreement is *openness*: we have to learn to be open to difference, to allow our pre-judgements to be challenged; in so doing we learn how to amend our assumptions, and develop an enriched understanding of others. It is precisely in confronting other beliefs and presuppositions that we are led to see the inadequacies of our own and transcend them. Rationality, in this perspective, is the willingness to admit the existence of better options, to be aware that one's knowledge is always open to refutation or modification from the vantage point of a different perspective. For Gadamer, the concept of 'bildung' describes the process through which individuals and communities enter a more and more widely defined community—they learn through dialogue to take a wider, more differentiated view, and thus acquire sensitivity, subtlety and capacity for judgement.

Reason emerges through dialogue with others, through which we learn not necessarily 'facts' but rather a capacity for learning, for new ways of thinking, speaking, and acting. It is Habermas (1979) who articulates the conditions for such communicative rationality as being 'ideal speech contexts' in which the participants feel able to speak freely, truly, sincerely. The conditions for this depend upon the creation of arenas for public discourse—the final and most significant condition for the creation of the learning society.

Conditions in the Polity

The conditions for a learning society are, in the last resort, fundamentally political, requiring the creation of a polity which provides the foundation for personal and collective empowerment (Sen 1990, 1992). The personal and social conditions described above will be hollow unless bedded in a conception of a reformed, more accountable, and thus more legitimate, political order. The connection between individual wellbeing and the vitality of the moral community is made in the public domain of the polity: the good (learning) person is a good citizen. Without political structures which bring together communities of discourse, the conditions for learning will not exist: it is not possible to create the virtues of learning without the forms of life and institutions which sustain them. The preconditions for the good polity are justice, participative democracy and public action, which I shall deal with in turn.

Justice: A Contract for the Basic Structure

The conditions for agency of self and society depend upon agreement about its value as well as about allocating the means for private and public self-determination. Freedom rests upon justice, as Rawls (1971) argues. But this makes the most rigorous demands upon the polity which has to determine the very conditions on which life can be lived at all: membership, the distribution of rights and duties, the allocation of scarce resources, the ends to be pursued—the good polity must strive to establish the conditions for virtue in all its citizens. These issues are intrinsically political and will be intensely contested, especially in a period of transformation that disturbs traditions and conventions.

Participative Democracy

Basing the new order upon the presupposition of agency leads to the principle of the equal rights of citizens both to participate in determining what conditions the expansion of their powers and to share responsibility for the common good. The political task of our time is to develop the polity as a vehicle for the active involvement of its citizens enabling them to make their contribution to the development of the learning society. There is a need, in this age of transition, to fashion a stronger, more active democracy than the post-war period has allowed. The post-war polity specialised politics and held the public at bay except periodically and passively. By providing forums for participation the new polity can create the conditions for public discourse and for mutual accountability so that citizens can take each others' needs and claims into account. Learning as discourse must underpin the learning society as the defining condition of the public domain.

Public Action

A more active citizenship, Mill believed, would be a civilising force in society. Through participation citizens would be educated in intellect, in virtue and in practical activity. The upshot of participation should now be public action based upon deeper consent than that obtained from earlier generations. For Sen (1990; Dreze and Sen 1989) the possibility of producing a fairer world, one which will enrich the capacities and entitlements of all citizens, depends upon the vitality of public, democratic action. The creation of a learning society expresses a belief in the virtue of the public domain and will depend upon the vitality of public action for its realisation. Education will always 'fail' if the capacity of young people has to be sectioned off to match a pyramidal, hierarchical society (the hidden curriculum of which is learned very early by young people), underpinned by a political system that encourages passive rather than active participation in the public domain. A different polity, enabling all people to make a purpose of their lives, will create the conditions for motivation in the classroom. Only a new moral and political order can provide the foundation for sustaining the personal development of all. It will encourage individuals to value their active role as citizens and thus their shared responsibility for the common-wealth. Active learning in the classroom needs, therefore, to be informed by and lead towards active citizenship within a participative democracy. Teachers and educational managers, with their deep understanding of the processes of learning, can, I believe, play a leading role in *enabling* such a vision to unfold not only among young people but also across the public domain.

Reforming Government for the Learning Society

The structure of government will need reforming if it is to enable the learning society. What framework of government is therefore appropriate to the needs of the learning society? I will consider the organising principles for a new framework and then set out the functions and powers of the tiers of government within a new structure of partnership.

The government of education should be constituted according to the following principles of organisation:

For the Public Good

Education is a public service constituted to enable an educated and educating public domain—open, just and democratic, respecting and involving the capacities of all citizens. The organising of education can facilitate or frustrate the creation of an open learning society. Private education denies the possibility of such a polity: it divides the educating of young people, so that those in the 'independent' sector acquire a hidden curriculum of power, a closed world behind the boundaries of protected exclusiveness. Respect and mutual co-operation cannot be developed in a polity where young people are segregated in their education along the class divide. Guidelines for the government of the learning society need to begin by celebrating education as a public good and challenging the enclaves of private power to take down the boundaries.

Enabling Participation for Civic Purpose

The challenge for education as it approaches the twenty-first century is to enable the public as citizens to contribute to the development of their own society. If equality and quality are to be assured then decisions about institutional arrangements, resourcing, staffing and curriculum development need to flow from a process of democratic and co-operative planning between the partners. Public choice needs planning if the results are to reflect the needs of all. The task is to discover a solution which eschews either professional corporatism or market self-interest and this challenge of realising public choice which is sensitive to diversity can only find its solution in processes that are much more democratic as well as collaborative than we have accomplished hitherto. The creation of community forums, councils and advisory panels can enable public discourse and tie participation into the processes of representative democracy.

Progressive Decentralisation

The relations between central and local government should be guided by the principle of progressive decentralisation in order to allow greater participation at every level in the government of the learning society. And yet if the principles of a new polity and society are to be accomplished, authority will need to be organised appropriately at every level, though according to the principle of subsidiarity with decision always taken at the lowest tier commensurate with efficiency. We need to be clear about the tasks to be undertaken as well as to have an understanding of the limits of government at different tiers: in short we need a theory of power and authority which analyses the distribution of powers to different tiers to fit their appropriate responsibilities and tasks.

☐ at the centre power is needed to determine the infrastructure of national public policy in education: its purposes, its learning principles, its frameworks, its resourcing, and its role in inspection and quality assurance;

☐ at the level of local governance, power is needed for the strategic planning and development of the systems of learning, institutional frameworks, networks of participation, public dialogue and quality assurance;

☐ at the level of institutions within the community, power is needed to enable local partnerships to form in support of individual and community participation to discuss and negotiate an education which empowers them as citizens. The powers of each of the other tiers of government have their rationale in enabling vitality of learning and participation at this level.

Thus responsibilities and powers should be distributed to each interdependent tier of education—the centre, the local authority, institutions and the community—so that each can make its appropriate contribution to shared overall purposes of the learning society by enabling autonomy and citizenship through a system of comprehensive and equal opportunities. The burden of power distribution is towards decentralisation but also towards partnership and mutual answerability.

Multiple Accountability

The principles of polycentrism and partnership from the period of social democracy need to be restored and further developed in any reformed government of education. The bureaucratic centralisation constituted by the ERA needs to give way to the understanding once more that public services need to acknowledge plural centres of power—centre, locality, institutions and the community—which must collaborate if the needs of all are to be met. The new partnerships require greater commitment than in the past to co-operative working and also to multiple accountability: willingness both to give an account of purposes and to be held to account on the exercise of responsibilities. What implications do these several organising principles have for a new structure to the government of education?

The Centre

A new Department of Education and Training should be created to integrate the functions of personal and skill development now divided between two Whitehall departments—the DE and the DFE. Even from a labour market perspective individuals require a much broader conception of continuing development at an advanced level if they are to provide for the needs of the emerging high tech service economy. At present, each department, without the proper influence of the other, will inevitably encourage too narrow a conception of the capacities needed for personal development, will duplicate innovation and deny integrated accountability.

The distinctive function of central government is to develop the purposes, principles and structures which provide the necessary conditions for the development of the learning society. The task for the centre is to prepare the national framework, the infrastructure for quality and equality in education rather than to prescribe the detail of institutional form or the content of the learning process. These are the proper responsibilities of the LEA and the teachers working in partnership with parents and the community. The primary *functions* of the centre therefore are to enable and promote national policy for the learning society, develop the infrastructure, develop strategic planning and resourcing, commission research and evaluate the quality of learning.

The classical view of the DFE has emphasised its role in the *promotion* of national policy. More recently, Glennerster (1990) has supported the effective impact of the department upon the climate of opinion in education 'through a rather intangible but very real shift in the balance of prevailing values'. What is now to be promoted? A principal task for the new DET should be to use this proven capacity to shape opinion and values by promoting the very notion of public education.

The department will have an essential role in coordinating the development of national policy. But because the education service must inescapably work through partnership the task of the centre is often to *enable* the partners to contribute to and share in the creation of national policy. Two organisational developments need consideration to supplement this role of the DET. First, whether there is a need to recreate the Advisory Councils (Robbins, Newsom, Plowden, etc.) which were a progressive influence in post-war education policy. The function of these councils is, at key moments, to draw together the disparate policy community in education to create a common language and shared understanding of the key policy issues. Whitehall would complain that this process is too slow, but the agreed proposals would prove longer lasting than instant policy-making in the heat of the political moment. Second, there will be a need to create a new integrated National Curriculum and Assessment Council, representative of the partners and radically revised in responsibilities. Curricula need to be adapted to meet the needs of the learner and thus to be open to the informed judgement of the local partners about the desired ideas and practices which should influence the curriculum. The proper role of the DFE is to establish principles which form a framework for learning: for example the values of educational purpose, the aims of learning, the curriculum design, assessment and pastoral care and counselling.

The centre, therefore, has an important task to enable the

partners to reach agreement about the characteristics and qualities of learning and then in generating understanding of good practice. The role of the centre is then to promote those ideas, innovations and practices which have been developed by teachers and LEAs to reform the quality of learning in schools, colleges and the community. The challenge for the department is to help stimulate and circulate the creative reforms which invariably grow up from the roots of the service.

A New Infrastructure

The role of promotion will in this way complement and reinforce the department's major function to constitute the infrastructure nationally for public comprehensive education. The following policies will be required to dissolve the market and regenerate the conditions for educational equality:

- end the grant maintained/CTC sector
- phase out the private sector
- end the voluntary sector

The most difficult task for the new DET will be to forge a settlement between the state and the private and voluntary sectors. Richard Pring (1987) has described the various ways in which private schooling is subsidised by public funds. There are obvious forms of state subsidy through the charitable status of independent schools which exempt them from paying taxes (on profit from fees) or national insurance (exemption from employers' surcharge) and gains them rate relief. Even more indirect support comes from the charitable status of non-educational institutions which can support private schools, or the corporate sector purchasing fees and places at such schools for their employees. A new settlement that began by offering financial incentives to the private sector to join the public sector would progressively reduce such subsidising of independent schooling.

Butler's compromise between church and state in 1944 was a major achievement. But there is growing understanding of the need for the state to review the settlement with the voluntary sector because of the problems caused by falling school rolls as well as the growth of multi-faith, multicultural society. In the past *The Times Educational Supplement* (1982) argued that there was a need to prepare the ground for new legislation later in the decade. The argument for change derives from the need to establish democratic control over a sector that can operate hidden selective admission policies, while the need to create a multicultural society would seem to require either that all the faiths can opt for denominational schooling or that all should give up their independence in the interests of a more integrated, though plural, society. The latter option now presents the stronger claims.

While the accelerating centralisation of power in Whitehall needs to end and be significantly reversed, it is nevertheless appropriate for the DFE to be accorded the necessary 'steering capacity' to implement agreed national policy. There is a need to restore the process of strategic development planning between central and local government. All LEAs would be required to submit to the DFE a plan for the development of education in their area. The plan would include a statement of strategic policy objectives for: the aims of the service; reforming teaching and learning; a design for curriculum and assessment; the pattern of institutional organisation; and how they intend to involve parents and community. Post-16 continuing education and training would be expected to form a large part of the development plan.

The plans would conform to a cycle of the kind the DFE has recommended for school development planning (DES 1989) and which is now widely regarded as good practice: they would be negotiated with the department which should require that they comply with the principles and guidelines expressed in national policy. The DFE would not be involved in determining the detail of plans. While it could require an LEA to have a policy plan which followed guidelines on equal opportunities it could not define the detailed programme. By controlling the process, the DFE would seek to encourage good practice. Where exemplary practice emerged the DES could work with these LEAs in order to develop understanding of the policies and practices for national dissemination. The DFE would continue to use Educational Specific Grants to promote and steer good practice locally.

Research is vital to the quality of progress within the education service. Policy developments in the service should always be underpinned by the knowledge and understanding provided by major research. (The Research Branch of the Inner London Education Authority was a national institution informing the educational community as a whole.) The DFE needs to establish an education research council which can sponsor major programmes of research into issues of equality, teaching and learning, community education, professional development, etc.

Monitoring and evaluating the quality of learning and institutional performance must be central to the education service at all levels. The process of external evaluation requires local authorities and their institutions to submit their practice to the critical examination of inspectors. The process of inspection ensures that practice is compared to the best experience elsewhere and that practice is made public and accountable to the wider community.

HM Inspectorate provided an invaluable service and needs to be restored. Its judgement was widely respected and its quasi-independence has been used to make challenging comments about the quality of education nationally as well as locally. The publicising of reports has strengthened its public influence: a critical account can prompt the partners to swift remedial action. HMI, however, was a professional body. There is a need for its work to be complemented and extended by a Quality Council. Such a Council, representative of the partners, would enable a national and public debate about achievement and performance in education. Its debates would draw upon research as well as the reports of inspectors.

The extraordinary extension of powers sanctioned by the 1988 Education Act needs to be reversed. Unlimited power in Whitehall contradicts the move towards a more participatory democracy. The centre needs those powers which are appropriate to its functions of establishing the purposes and infrastructures of the nation's public education service—but not powers to intervene in detail.

Thus retaining Section 1 of the 1944 Education Act, without powers of detailed intervention, restores the relationship between central and local government that obtained prior to the mid-1970s. That is, the department was required to work in partnership with local government because although it had overall responsibility it could not determine the detail. Civil servants complained that this was intolerable because it provided them with authority bereft of power and it made for slow implementation of change. Nevertheless, partnership is better than authoritarian centralism, and time for consultation is the beneficial price of accountable democracy.

Local Government

The central questions facing the reform of educational government surround the LEA: should local government have a role in education and, if so, what should be its proper functions? In the period of social democracy the LEA became arguably the key arm of planning post-war reforms, in particular the movement for creating a comprehensive system of schools that would enable all young people to experience educational, and thus career opportunities, previously reserved for a privileged minority. LEAs saw their role as providing the buildings, staff and resources that would establish the infrastructure of opportunities for teachers to practise their professional skills within schools and colleges aimed at developing the powers and capacities of young people. The LEA, as the 'maintaining' or 'providing' LEA, had wide-ranging responsibilities for providing a comprehensive service in its area not only for the three stages of learning—primary, secondary and further—but also for the community as a whole ('to contribute towards the spiritual, moral, mental and physical development of the community, by securing that efficient education throughout those stages shall be available to meet the needs of the population of their area' [S7 1944 Education Act]). Although the LEA had responsibility for the curriculum (S27 1944 Act) issues of learning process were typically regarded as professional matters for heads and their teaching staffs in schools and colleges. LEAs developed and administered the framework of education while delegating the content and quality of learning to others.

The achievement of the 1988 Education Reform Act was to propose that this traditional focus was now misplaced and the energies of the LEA, if it was to have any role in the future scheme of things, ought to concentrate upon ensuring the quality of learning in schools and colleges—by monitoring and evaluating the implementation of the National Curriculum. Learning quality and accountability to parents and the public were now the primary functions of the LEA rather than directly providing and administering services. A continuing strategic role of leading the system was open to the LEA if it could achieve the confidence of schools, colleges and the community. Whereas the traditional role of the LEA was to provide and maintain the administrative and institutional infrastructures for schools and colleges, now the overriding mission of the local education authority is to reform the process of learning, enhance the quality of achievement and promote a new relationship of service and accountability to the public. These values are complemented by a new understanding of management as strategic leadership of a service founded upon partnership.

Recent research (Ranson 1992; Cordingley and Kogan 1993) suggests that local government has a quite indispensable role to play in developing equality of opportunity and quality of learning in a democratic society. While future reforms can build upon the positive developments contained within the 1988 Education Reform Act some of the functions and constitutive powers need to be restored to the local government of education to enable it to fulfil a more powerful brief than accorded to it in recent legislation. The case for the local government of education rests upon three arguments:

☐ that learning is inescapably a *system*: learning is a process which cannot be contained within the boundaries of any one institution. Discovery and understanding occur at home, in the community, on a scheme of work experience as well as in college or school. Progress, furthermore, will unfold more securely between stages of learning when they are mutually comprehending and supporting. Improving achievement, it is proposed, depends for its realisation upon enabling a wider system of learning: one element cannot be treated in isolation from another if each is to contribute to the effective working of the whole. Ensuring, for every school, the appropriate numbers of pupils, and the provision of resources and teachers to support a balanced and comprehensive curriculum with choices at key stages to enable progression in response to diversity of need, are characteristics which have to be managed at the level of the system as a whole, as well as that of the school, if all young people are to be provided with opportunities to realise their powers and capacities.

☐ education needs to be a local system: the system of learning is more effective if managed locally, as well as nationally and at the level of the institution. The different tasks need their appropriate tier of management and by creating a local system which delegated and enabled strategic leadership, the 1988 reforms enacted the conditions for excellence in the local management of education within a national framework. A local system of management is needed to ensure understanding of local needs, responsiveness to changing circumstances, and efficiency in the management of resources within geographic boundaries consistent with identifiable historic traditions. Such local systems need to be properly accountable and this requires location within a local democratic system.

☐ education needs to be a local *democratic* system: if education is, as it should be, a public service of and for the whole community rather than merely the particular parents, young people and employers who have an immediate and proper interest in the quality of the education provided, then education must be responsive and accountable to the community as a whole. The significance of learning for the public as a whole suggests the indispensable location of the service within a framework of democratic local government which enables all local people to express their views and to participate actively in developing the purposes and processes of their education service. A learning society—enabling all to contribute to and respond to the significant changes of the period—will depend for its vitality upon the support of local democratic institutions which articulate and take responsibility for developing all members of community.

A flourishing public domain requires the vitality which local democratic governance brings to education. Upon local authorities lies the inescapable task of both reinterpreting national purpose to local need and generating the shared sense of purpose that is the precondition for public confidence and commitment. Only a very sophisticated social institution could bring off this demanding task. The challenge for the future is to extend rather than extinguish the qualities of equality and justice which local democracy should encompass.

Structures

New reforms need first to celebrate the principle of local democracy and government of education, as the previous section argued. The LEA is not a tier of administration, nor a separate tier: it is an integral part of a major institution of democracy in our society. Education will benefit from stronger rather than weaker local government. To this end the multi-purpose local authority of the kind proposed by the Redcliffe Maud Commission Report in 1969 should be established to restore the links between town and country, incorporating health and water, and to have 'an all round responsibility for the safety, health and well-being, both material and cultural, of people in their locality'. The focus of this strengthened local government would be upon the strategic planning and development of the public services within its area including school and college building, hospitals, housing, environmental health and other services. The functions of the strategic authority would be to establish the infrastructure, the foundations for more participation within the community. At this level representative democracy draws together the diversity of local perspectives and ensures collective decisions for action that are clear, legitimate and accountable.

The local education authority is central to the vision of this new strategic local government. Its task is to prepare a development plan which both articulates the purposes of the national framework and also expresses the ambitions for citizenship in the learning society as expressed within local communities and their institutions. This vision of the local government of education must constitute an integrated set of institutions serving local democratic education. Just as any national framework would make little sense if a local authority could opt out, so the local government of education fails to make any consistent sense if institutions are allowed to opt out at will. Members of the public domain cannot stand outside their responsibilities for the public domain. The challenge for the future is for all to make attractive and rewarding the public space in which all must live and flourish. If problems exist, as no doubt they will at a local level, in relationships between an authority, its institutions and the public, then they have to be addressed in other ways, as they are of course when they are experienced at a national level, in the appropriate procedures and tribunals of public accountability.

This structure constitutes a much more complex network of participation in decision-making than hitherto. Although the reformed local government of education will restore its institutional unity and coherence, the tradition of hierarchical control will remain a thing of the past. The local authority will relate to a more diffuse system of councils, institutions and agencies, and although it will be accorded greater 'steering capacity' than under the 1988 Education Reform Act it must, nevertheless, largely seek to influence and to work in partnership with rather than direct. But this is to begin to describe the functions of the new LEA.

Functions

The primary purpose of the local government of education is to enable the unfolding of the learning society within an LEA area of responsibility. Its task is to provide strategic leadership that will encourage the local education partners to develop a shared under-standing of learning quality, of the system of management and of public service and accountability.

Vision of Learning

The functions of the LEA in developing the system of learning can be summarised once more as follows: working within the national framework, to develop a vision of equality and quality in educational opportunity for all in society throughout their lives, one that will celebrate diversity of culture; to secure a learning context free from prejudice and discrimination, and a commitment of institutions to social justice; to reform the organisation and process of learning so as to give all students access to a broad and balanced curriculum through strategies which encourage active and flexible approaches to learning and progression in learning within and between the stages of learning.

The LEA therefore has a leading role to play in generating understanding of and the conditions for processes of learning that will release the powers and capacities of adults as well as young people and encourage them to make their responsible contribution to the development of their society.

Strategic Planning and Resourcing

The LEA has the key function of ensuring that there is cohesion and direction to the promotion of the local vision of education through the articulation of interdependent development plans from every part of the service which express specific objectives while taking account of the local authority's mission. In this way LEA policy statements about, for example, supporting the special learning needs of the disadvantaged can be given expression and resource advantage throughout the service as a whole. It will be a key role of the local government of education to approve the development plans for the constituent parts of the service.

Resource distribution throughout the education authority will reflect the policy objectives expressed in the strategic plan with specific grants targeting chosen priorities for innovation and development. Formulas for funding institutions and centres will be calculated on the basis of need rather than the *per capita* (quasi voucher) system implemented in the Education Reform Act.

LEAs will also ensure efficient provision of services, evaluate quality, develop partnerships and enable participation and voice in education from parents, employers and the wider public. Together these functions of the local government of education identify an increasingly complex challenge of facilitating a much more enriched conception of the learning society than has been the case traditionally: one which facilitates the responsible participation of citizens, a culture of deliberation and action for the common good as well as personal development.

Powers

Although the LEA should not return to a mode of detailed and hierarchical administrative control of the local education service, it should be a unified although differentiated service, and should be accorded appropriate capacity to steer the system as a whole in just the same way as Whitehall should be accorded steering capacity to ensure some unity as well as diversity in the national education service.

The LEAs' deployment of such powers will grow in authority and legitimacy the more the policies which they seek to implement are derived in association with the local partners so that there is a shared understanding of the purposes and plans for development of the service as a whole.

Institutions

Any programme of reforms to the local government of education needs to build upon the achievements of the 1988 Education Reform Act in strengthening the authority and quality of schools and colleges. But the emphasis in that legislation on encouraging schools and colleges to see themselves as isolated, inward-looking islands of learning, needs to be dissolved in favour of values which support the contribution the institution can make to learning in the life of the community as a whole. Schools and colleges need, as some already have, to form local institutional networks of learning in partnership with parents and the community to support the more inspiring vision of the learning society.

A number of values are already established objectives for schools and colleges: what is offered in terms of opportunities, resources and facilities. Thus it can be argued that provision should enable the principles of: *entitlement* to a comprehensive and continuing education for all to achieve personal growth throughout their lives; *responsivesness* to the expressed educational needs of all in the community; *accessibility* to enable members of the community to take up learning opportunities, which require *flexibility* of provision in schools and especially in further and higher education to enable students to transfer courses and maintain *progression* in learning. *Resources* remain a vital condition for educational quality and these LEAs invested considerably in staff development; indeed they strove to protect expenditure in the face of pressure to contract it. A belief in *quality development* was expressed in the growing commitment to the monitoring and evaluation of provision. Teachers and advisers sought to develop principles which would encourage a *comprehensive curriculum* that would be relevant to learners, enabling them to draw upon their experience of living within the community. This proposed curriculum should be broad and balanced in the learning offered, modular in its form, though ensuring coherence and integration across the experience of learning, enabling continuity and progression, and supporting young people with formative and positive assessment to help them understand their achievements and progress.

If learning is to be effective it should motivate young people by engaging their interest and by being related to their experience. The process of teaching, moreover, should seek to involve students in, and negotiate with them, a process of active and collaborative learning: 'we must shift from a teaching approach to a learning approach'.

Parents and the Community

The purpose of all the reforms is to enable a learning society, one in which parents are as much committed to their own continuing development as they are to supporting their children's unfolding education, in which women assert their right to learn as well as support the family, in which learning co-operatives are formed at work and in community centres, and in which all are preoccupied with the issues of purpose and organisation of learning enough to get involved in the public dialogue about reform.

Such a participative democracy in and for education presupposes a strong 'periphery' to education as it does a strong LEA or state. Indeed, in the new order of things, the periphery should be perceived as the centre with all the other tiers of government seen as circles of enabling support radiating out from the defining purpose of it all— ordinary people individually and together devoting their energies to developing their own powers and capacities but also those of the local community. Taking responsibility for the quality of the common- wealth is an intrinsic value as well as being a condition for the autonomy of each.

Schools and colleges are part of such a strong area and community perspective, committed to working together so that they are more effective in listening to and responding to the articulated needs of the community. Organisation is a vehicle for purpose and if the principle of participation and local responsiveness is to be firmly established then organisational mechanisms need to be developed to support the identification of local needs, facilitate participation and support the coordination of schools, colleges and centres. These mechanisms could take three forms:

Community Forums

Some schools have in the past introduced such forums to extend community participation, and in some authorities forums have been established for specific purposes, for example to review proposals for school reorganisation, or more generally to consider educational issues. A stronger democracy suggests the need for community forums with a wider remit to enable parents, employers and community groups to express local needs and share in decision-making about provision to meet them.

Grant-giving Capacity

Public dialogue about educational reform is properly a primary responsibility of community forums, but they should be able to exert influence, and a limited resource-giving capacity (delegated by the local authority) could be deployed in support of the learning needs of individuals and groups within the community. This would be an important strategy in enfranchising and empowering community education and reinforce the providers' responsiveness to local needs.

The Enabling Role of the Area Officer

The mutual co-operation of schools, colleges and centres in support of the learning society will sometimes happen spontaneously. It is likely to be accelerated with the support area officer or adviser who encourages parental and group involvement in identifying learning needs and in deciding upon and organising appropriate development projects. Monitoring and evaluating progress, enabling the dialogue of accountability, are crucial activities in the role.

It is a networking role, in which the officer, or local community representative, works to link up the parts of the service so that the local authority and its institutions can make an integrated response to the needs of parents and the community. The officer becomes the 'animateur' of the community as an educational campus.

Conclusion

A reformed government of education is needed to support the needs of a new age for a learning society in which all can develop and contribute their powers and capacities. Education will always 'fail' if the capacity of young people has to be sectioned off to match a pyramidal, hierarchical society underpinned by a political system that encourages passive rather than active participation in the public domain. A different polity, enabling all people to make a purpose of their lives, will create the conditions for motivation in the classroom. Only a new moral and political order can provide the foundation for sustaining the personal development of all. It will encourage individuals to value their active role as citizens and thus their shared responsibility for the common-wealth. Active learning in the classroom needs, therefore, to be informed by and lead towards active citizenship within a participative democracy. Teachers and educational managers, with their deep understanding of the processes of learning, can, I believe, play a leading role in enabling such a vision to unfold not only among young people but also across the public domain.

NOTES AND REFERENCES

Introduction

Sally Tomlinson

1. As of February 1994 there were some 814 (out of 24,000) grant-maintained schools. A Conservative minister stated in the House of Commons that 'half a million parents have voted to become GM in ballots' (*Hansard* 1 March 1994, vol.238, no.58, p.861). However this is fewer than 7 per cent of all parents with children in schools (assuming two parents equal one child).

References

Department for Education (1992) *Choice and Diversity*. cmnd, 2021, London: DFE (white paper).

IPPR (1993) *Education: A Different Vision*. London: Institute for Public Policy Research.

Green, A. and Steedman, H. (1993) *Educational Provision, Educational Attainment and the Needs of Industry: A Review of Research for Germany, Japan, France, the USA and Britain*. London: National Institute for Economic and Social Research.

Labour Party (1993) *Opening Doors to a Learning Society—An Alternative Green Paper on Education*. London: Labour Party.

Reich, R. (1991) *The Work of Nations*. New York: Simon and Schuster.

Sayer, J. (1993) *The Future Governance of Education*. London: Cassell.

The Times (1992) Editorial, 29 July 1992.

Tomlinson, S. (1993) 'Education: Vision, Principles and Policies'. *Renewal*, vol.1, no.4, pp.47–56.

1 Market Forces and Parental Choice

Stephen J. Ball, Richard Bowe and Sharon Gewirtz

Ball, S.J., Bowe, R. and Gewirtz, S. (1995) 'Circuits of Schooling: A Sociological Exploration of Parental Choice of School in Social Class Contexts.' *Sociological Review*, forthcoming.

Ball, S.J. (1993) Education Markets, Choice and Social Class: The Market as a Class Strategy in the UK and the USA.' *British Journal of Sociology of Education* 14(1): pp.3–20.

Beck, U. (1992) *The Risk Society: Towards a New Modernity*. London: Sage.

Bourdieu, P. (1986) *Distinction: A Social Critique of the Judgement of Taste*. London: Routledge and Kegan Paul.

Bowe, R., Ball, S.J., Gewirtz, S. (1993) 'Captured by the Discourse? Issues and Concerns in Researching "Parental Choice"': *British Journal of Sociology of Education* 15(1): pp.63–78.

Daunt, P. (1975) *Comprehensive Values*. London: Heinemann.

Department for Education (1992) *Choice and Diversity: A New Framework for Schools*. London: HMSO.

Featherstone, M. (1992) *Consumer Culture and Postmodernism*. London: Sage.

Gewirtz, S., Ball, S.J., and Bowe, R. (1994). 'Values and Ethics in the Education Market Place: The Case of Northwark Park.' *International Studies in the Sociology of Education*, 3, 2, pp.235–54.

Gewirtz, S., Ball, S.J. and Bowe, R. (1994) 'Parents, Privilege and the Education Market.' *Research Papers in Education*, forthcoming.

Kemeny, J. (1992) *Housing and Social Structure: Towards a Sociology of Residence*. Bristol: SAUS Publications.

Kingdom, J. (1992) *No Such Thing as Society? Individualism and Community*. Buckingham: Open University Press.

Lowery, D., de Hoog, R. and Lyons, W.E. (1992) 'Citizenship in the Empowered Locality.' *Urban Affairs Quarterly* 28(1), pp.69–103.

Nagel, T. (1991) *Equality and Partiality*. Oxford: Oxford University Press.

2 Underpinning Choice and Diversity?

Sally Power, David Halpin and John Fitz

The authors gratefully acknowledge the support of the Economic and Social Research Council (Award No.R000231899) for the research reported in this paper.

References

Anon (1992) 'Preventing school fiefdoms.', *Independent*, 22 February.

Ashworth, J., Papps, I. and Thomas, B. (1988) *Increased Parental Choice.* Warlingham: Institute of Economic Affairs Education Unit.

Baker, K. (1987) Parliamentary Debates, *Proceedings of the House of Commons*, 1 December, Column 778.

Ball, S.J. (1990) *Education, Inequality and School Reform: Values in Crisis!* Inaugural Lecture, King's College, University of London.

Ball, S.J., Bowe, R. and Gewirtz, S. (1995) 'Circuits of Schooling: A Sociological Exploration of Parental Choice in Social Class Contexts' *Sociological Review*, forthcoming 1995

Bowe, R., Ball, S.J. with Gold, A. (1992) *Reforming Education and Changing Schools: Case Studies in Policy Sociology*. London, Routledge.

Brehony, K.J. (1992) "Active Citizens': the Case of School Governors.' *International Studies in Sociology of Education*, 2 (2), pp.199–217.

Bush, T., Coleman, M. and Glover, D. (1993) *Managing Autonomous Schools: The Grant-Maintained Experience*. London: Paul Chapman.

Centre for Policy Studies (1988), 'Advice to the Education Secretary.' In Haviland, J. *Take Care Mr Baker!* London: Fourth Estate.

Chubb, J.E. and Moe, T.M. (1990) *Politics, Markets and America's Schools*. Washington DC: Brookings Institute.

Conservative Party (1992) *Better Schools—Better Standards* London: Conservative and Unionist Central Office.

Deem, R., Brehony, K.J. and Hemmings, S. (1991) 'Social Justice, Social Divisions and the Governing of Schools', in Gill, D. and Mayor, B. (eds) *Racism and Education: Structures and Strategies*. London. Sage.

Deem, R. and Wilkins, J. (1992) 'Governing and Managing Schools after ERA: the LEA experience and the GMS Alternative'. in Simkins, T., Ellison, L. and Garrett, V. (eds) *Implementing Educational Reform: The Early Lessons*. Harlow: Longman.

Department for Education (1992) *Choice and Diversity—A New Framework for Schools*. London: Department for Education.

Edwards, T., Fitz, J. and Whitty, G. (1989) *The State and Private Education: An Evaluation of the Assisted Places Scheme*. London: Falmer Press.

Edwards, T. and Whitty, G. (1992) 'Parental Choice and Educational Reform in Britain and the United States.' *British Journal of Educational Studies*, 50 (2), pp.101–17.

Edwards, T., Gewirtz, S. and Whitty, G. (1992a) 'City Technology Colleges and Curriculum Innovation'. Paper presented to *Parental Choice and Market Forces Seminar 2*, King's College, London, 31 January.

Edwards, T., Gewirtz, S. and Whitty, G. (1992b) 'Researching a Policy in Progress: The City Technology Colleges Initiative'. *Research Papers in Education* 7 (1) pp.79–104.

Fitz, J., Power, S. and Halpin, D. (1993a) 'Opting for Grant-Maintained Status: A Case Study of Policy-making in Education'. *Policy Studies*, 14 (1) pp.4–20.

Fitz, J., Halpin, D. and Power, S. (1993b) *Grant-Maintained Schools: Education in the Marketplace*. London: Kogan Page.

Flew, A. (1991) 'Educational Services: Independent Competition or Maintained Monopoly.' in Green, D.G. (ed.) *Empowering the Parents: How to Break the Schools Monopoly* London, Institute of Economic Awareness Health and Welfare Unit.

Ford, J. (1969) *Social Class and the Comprehensive School*. London: Routledge and Kegan Paul.

Golby, M. and Brigley, S. (1989) *Parents as School Governors*. Tiverton: Fair Way Publications.

Goldthorpe, J. and Hope, K. (1974) *The Social Grading of Occupations: A New Approach and Scale*. Oxford: Clarendon Press.

Halpin, D. and Fitz, J. (1990) 'Researching Grant-maintained Schools', *Journal of Education Policy*. 5 (2), pp.167–80.

Halpin, D., Power, S. and Fitz, J. (1994) 'Opting into State Control? Headteachers and the Paradoxes of Grant-maintained Status'. *International Studies in the Sociology of Education*, 3(1).

Hillgate Group (1986) *Whose Schools? A Radical Manifesto* London: Hillgate Group.

Hirsch, F. (1977) *Social Limits to Growth*. London: Routledge and Kegan Paul.

Hirschmann, A. (1970) *Exit, Voice and Loyalty*. Cambridge: Harvard University Press.

Jackson, B. and Marsden, D. (1962) *Education and the Working Class*. London: Routledge and Kegan Paul.

Mason, P. (1992) *Independent Education in Western Europe*, ISIS Document no.34 London: Independent Schools Information Service.

Miliband, D. (1991) *Markets, Politics and Education: Beyond the Education Reform Act*. London: Institute for Public Policy Research.

No Turning Back Group (1986) *Save Our Schools*. London: Conservative Political Centre.

Patten, C. (1993) Secretary of State's speech to the Grant-Maintained Schools Centre Conference, Birmingham, 29 March.

Raywid, M.A. (1985) 'Family Choice Arrangements in Public Schools: A Review of the Literature.' *Review of Educational Research*, 55, pp.435–67.

Rogers, M. (1992) *Opting out: Choice and the Future of Schools*. London: Lawrence and Wishart.

Rumbold, A. (1989) Parliamentary Debates, *Proceedings of the House of Commons*, 3 March, Column 337.

Rumbold, A. (1990) Parliamentary Debates, *Proceedings of the House of Commons*, 12 June, Column 128.

Sexton, S. (1989) *Opting to Grant Maintained Status*. London: Institute of Economic Affairs.

Tebbit, N. (1987) Parliamentary Debates, *Proceedings of the House of Commons*, 1 December, Column 812.

Vincent, C. (1993a) 'Education for the Community.' *British Journal of Educational Studies*, 41(4).

Vincent, C. (1993b) 'Community Participation? The Establishment of City's Parents' Centre', *British Educational Research Journal*, 19(3) 221–35.

Walford, G. and Miller, H. (1991) *City Technology College*. Milton Keynes: Open University Press.

Webster, A. (1993) *School Marketing: Making it Easy for Parents to Select your School*. Bristol: Avec Designs.

West, A., David, M., Hailes, J., Ribbens, J. and Hind, A. (1993) *Choosing a Secondary School: The Parents' and Pupils' Stories*, Clare Market Papers no.7. London: London School of Economics, Centre for Educational Research.

Whitty, G. (1989) 'The New Right and the National Curriculum: State Control or Market Forces?' *Journal of Education Policy* 4(4) pp.329–41.

Williams, R. (1971) *The Long Revolution*. London: Chatto and Windus.

Wohlstetter, P. and Anderson, L. (1992) 'What Can US Charter Schools Learn from England's Grant-Maintained Schools?' Paper presented at American Educational Research Association, San Francisco, April.

3 The Political Economy of Local Management of Schools

Hywel Thomas and Alison Bullock

1. The data reported in this paper were collected as part of a project funded by The Leverhulme Trust on *The Funding of Schools after the 1988 Education Reform Act*. We are pleased to acknowledge the support of the Trust.

2. A full discussion of allocative mechanisms in education is set out in a paper by Thomas, 1994.

3. Historic budgets were calculated for each school using the formula:
[(budshare—formula)/(level of transitional protection for 1990/91/100] + formula

4. In turning to consider the impact of the change to formula funding on schools with additional educational needs, we enter an initial caveat. Schools with additional needs are defined in terms of each LEA's own formula. That may mean that, on different criteria, other schools could be identified as having additional needs. We regard this internal comparison

167

as valid, on the basis that we are assessing the effect of an LEA's local interpretation of the national guidance.
5. The asterisks indicate level of confidence (that the association is not owing to chance):
   *   means confidence at the 0.05 level
   ** means confidence at the 0.01 level
   The closer the correlation is to 1, positive or negative, the stronger the association between the two variables.
6. Primary: r = 0.50**; Secondary: r = 0.40**
7. All schools: r = 0.04. Primary: r = 0.03. Secondary: r = -0.26
8. The 1986 Act strengthened the recruitment position of schools but left with LEAs the authority to place teachers in a school. Bullock, A. and Thomas, H. (1994) *The Funding of Schools after the 1988 Education Reform Act*: University of Birmingham.

References

Plant, R. (1990) 'Citizenship and Rights.' In *Citizenship and Rights in Thatcher's Britain: Two Views*. London: IEA Health and Welfare Unit.

Scottish Office (1992a) *Using Ethos Indicators in Secondary School Self-Evaluation: Taking Account of the Views of Pupils, Parents and Teachers*, HM Inspectors of Schools, Edinburgh, Scottish Office.

Scottish Office (1992b) *Using Ethos Indicators in Primary School Self-Evaluation: Taking Account of the Views of Pupils, Parents and Teachers*, HM Inspectors of Schools, Edinburgh, Scottish Office.

Thomas, H. (1994) 'Markets, Collectivities and Management.' *Oxford Review of Education*.

Titmuss, R.M. (1970) *The Gift Relationship*. London: Allen and Unwin.

Ware, A. (1990) 'Meeting Needs through Voluntary Action: Does Market Society Corrode Altruism?' In Ware, A. and Goodin, R.E. (eds) *Needs and Welfare*. London: Sage.

4 An Alternative National Curriculum

Philip O'Hear

Dearing, R (1994) *The National Curriculum and its Assessment*. London: Schools Curriculum and Assessment Authority.

O'Hear, P. and White, J. (1991) *A National Curriculum for All*, Education and Training Paper 6, London, Institute for Public Policy Research.

5 An Interim Approach to Unifying the Post-16 Curriculum

Michael Young, Annette Hayton, Ann Hodgson and Andrew Morris

The authors would like to thank their colleague Andy Green for his valuable comments on an earlier draft of this paper. They acknowledge the financial support of the Paul Hamlyn Foundation in the preparation of this paper.

Some of the ideas in this paper were presented by Michael Young and Andrew Morris to the Leverhulme Trust/IPPR conference on 'Alternative Education Policies' at the IBIS Hotel, 24–25 March 1993. The methodological issues concerning theory and practice were taken further in *A British Baccalauréat? Curriculum and Research Networks for Post Compulsory Education and Training* by Michael Young and Annette Hayton (forthcoming).

1. This distinction is made in order to problematise the relationship between those in universities, which are assumed to be the major sites of knowledge production, and teachers, and lecturers. It does not mean that those involved in curriculum delivery do not develop theory or that research may not be a practical activity.

2. The three key examples are:
   (i) The FEU Credit Accumulation and Transfer Network;
   (ii) The London Together initiative to develop a credit framework for London;
   (iii) The Higher Education Quality Council investigation into the possibilities of a credit framework to embrace further, adult and higher education.

References

CBI (1993) *Routes for Success*. London: Confederation of British Industries.

Finegold, D. *et al.* (1990) *A British Baccalauréat: Ending the Division between Education and Training*. London: Institute for Public Policy Research.

Finegold, D. and Soskice, D. (1988) 'The Failure of Training.' *Oxford Review of Economic Policy*, vol.4, no.3.

Government White Paper (1991) *Education and Training for the 21st century*, London: HMSO.

Morgan, G. (1988) *Images of Organisation*. London: Sage.

Morris, A. (1992) *Towards A Unified Curriculum at 16+*, Post-16 Education Centre Working Paper, no.12, University of London.

Spours, K. and Young, M. (1992) *A Curriculum for the Future*, Post-16 Education Centre discussion paper, University of London.

Young, M. (1993a) 'Modularisation and Outcomes: Towards a Strategy for a Curriculum for the Future.' In Burke, J. (ed.) *Outcomes and the Curriculum*, Falmer Press (forthcoming).

Young, M. (1993b) 'A Curriculum for the 21st Century: Towards a New Basis for Overcoming Academic-Vocational Divisions.' *British Journal of Educational Studies*, August, vol.XXXXI, no.3.

Young, M. and Watson, J. (eds) (1992) 'The Case for a Unified System at 16+.' Post-16 Education Centre Report, University of London.

6 Teacher Education and Teacher Competence

Pat Mahony and Geoff Whitty

This paper was originally presented at the IPPR–Goldsmiths' seminar on Alternative Education Policies at the Hotel Ibis, Euston, London, 25–26 March 1993. It has been modified to take account of subsequent changes in government policy up to January 1994. Some sections are based on a paper by Geoff Whitty on 'Education Reform and Teacher Education in England in the 1990s', which appeared in P. Gilroy and M. Smith (eds) *International Analyses of Teacher Education* (Oxford, Carfax 1993) and a paper by Susan Sidgwick, Pat Mahony and Ian Hextall, entitled 'Policy and Practice in the Professional Development of Teachers', which appeared in *International Studies in the Sociology of Education*, 3(2), 1993.

References

Ball, S. and Bowe, R. (1992) 'Subject departments and the "implement-ation" of National Curriculum policy; an overview of the issues'. *Journal of Curriculum Studies*, 24(2), pp.97–115.

Barrett, E., Barton, L., Furlong, J., Galvin, C., Miles, S. and Whitty, G. (1992) 'New Routes to Qualified Teacher Status'. *Cambridge Journal of Education*, 22(3), pp.323–5.

Barton, L., Pollard, A. and Whitty, G. (1992) 'Experiencing CATE: The Impact of Accreditation on Initial Teacher Training Institution'. *Journal of Education for Teaching*, 18(1), pp.41–57.

Booth, M., Furlong, J., Hargreaves, D., Reiss, M. and Ruthven, K. (1989) *Teacher Supply and Teacher Quality: Solving the Crisis*. Cambridge: University of Cambridge Department of Education.

Campaign for Real Education (1989) 'Cause for Concern'. *Campaign for Real Education Newsletter*, 3(1).

Dawson, G. (1981) 'Unfitting teachers to teach.' In Flew, A. *et al. The Pied Pipers of Education*. London: Social Affairs Unit.

DES (1984) *Initial Teacher Training: Approval of Courses* (Circular 3/84). London: Department of Education and Science.

DES (1989) *Initial Teacher Training: Approval of Courses* (Circular 24/89). London: Department of Education and Science.

DES (1992) *Reform of Initial Teacher Training: a consultation document.* London: Department of Education and Science.

DFE (1992) *Initial Teacher Training (Secondary Phase)* (Circular 9/92). London: Department for Education.

DFE (1993a) *The Government's Proposals for the Reform of Initial Teacher Training.* London: Department for Education.

DFE (1993b) *The Initial Training of Primary School Teachers: New Criteria for Course Approval* (Draft Circular). London: Department for Education.

DFE (1993c) *The Initial Training of Primary School Teachers* (Circular 14/93). London: Department for Education.

Gamble, A. (1983) 'Thatcherism and Conservative Politics' in Hall, S. and Jacques, M. (eds) *The Politics of Thatcherism.* London: Lawrence and Wishart.

Hargreaves, D. (1990) 'Another Radical Approach to the Reform of Initial Teacher Training'. *Westminster Studies in Education*, 13.

HMI (1989) The Provisional Teacher Program in New Jersey. London: HMSO.

HMI (1991) *School-based Initial Teacher Training in England and Wales.* London: HMSO.

Hextall, I., Lawn, M., Menter, I., Sidgwick, S. and Walker, S. (1991) *Imaginative Projects: Arguments for a New Teacher Education.* London: Goldsmiths' College.

Hillgate Group (1987) *The Reform of British Education.* London: Claridge Press.

Hillgate Group (1989) *Learning to Teach.* London: Claridge Press.

Holmes Group (1990) *Tomorrow's Schools: Principles for the Design of Professional Development Schools.* East Lansing: Holmes Group.

Lawlor, S. (1990) *Teachers Mistaught: Training in Theories or Education in Subjects?* London: Centre for Policy Studies.

Lawton, D. (1990) 'The Future of Teacher Education' in Graves, N. (ed.) *Initial Teacher Education: Policies and Progress* London: Kogan Page.

Maclure, S. (1993) 'Fight this tooth and nail'. *The Times Educational Supplement*, 18 June.

Marsland, D. (1992) *Towards the Renewal of British Education.* London: Campaign for Real Education.

McElvogue, M. and Salters, M. (1992) 'Models of Competence and Teacher Training.' Paper presented to UCET annual conference, Oxford, 13–15 November.

Munro, R. (1989) 'A Case Study of School-based Innovation in Secondary Teacher Training.' PhD Thesis, University of Auckland.

NCC (1991) *The National Curriculum and the Initial Training of Student, Articled and Licensed Teachers*. York: National Curriculum Council.

OFSTED (1993) *The Licensed Teacher Scheme September 1990–July 1992*. London: HMSO.

O'Hear, A. (1988) *Who Teaches the Teachers?* London: Social Affairs Unit.

O'Keeffe, D. (1990a) 'Equality and Childhood: Education and the Myths of Teacher Training.' In Graves, N. (ed.), *Initial Teacher Education: Policies and Progress*. London: Kogan Page.

O'Keeffe, D. (1990b) *The Wayward Elite*. London: Adam Smith Institute.

Pyke, N. (1993) 'Schools Seek Cash for Initial Training'. *The Times Educational Supplement*, 12 March.

Reid, K. and Newby, M. (1988) 'Is the Green Paper a Cheap Licence to Teach?' *Education*, 172(7).

Sidgwick, S. Mahony, P. and Hextall, I. (1993) 'Policy and Practice in the Professional Development of Teachers'. *International Studies in the Sociology of Education*, 3(2), pp.91–108.

Tomlinson, S. and Ross, A. (1991) *Teachers and Parents*. London: IPPR.

Whitty, G. (1989) 'The New Right and the National Curriculum: State Control or Market Forces?' *Journal of Education Policy*, 4(4), pp.329–41.

Whitty, G. (1990) 'The Politics of the Education Reform Act.' In Dunleavy, P., Gamble, A. and Peel, G. (eds) *Developments in British Politics 3*. London: Macmillan.

Whitty, G., Barrett, E., Barton, L., Furlong, J., Galvin, C., and Miles, S. (1992) 'Initial Teacher Education in England and Wales: A Survey of Current Practices and Concerns', *Cambridge Journal of Education*, 22(3), pp.293–306.

Whitty, G., Barton, L. and Pollard, A. (1987). 'Ideology and Control in Teacher Education.' In T. Popkewitz (ed.) *Critical Studies in Teacher Education*. Lewes: Falmer Press.

Whitty, G. and Willmott, E. (1991) 'Competence-based Teacher Education: Approaches and Issues.' *Cambridge Journal of Education*, 21(3), pp.309–18.

Wolf, A. (1989) 'Can Competence and Knowledge Mix?' in J.W. Burke (ed.) *Competency Based Education and Training*. Lewes: Falmer Press.

7 Alternative Education Policies: School Inspection

Eric Bolton

Bates, S. (1991) '"Sinister" School Inspections Changes Attacked' *Guardian*, 2 October 1991, p.2.

Lawlor, S. (1993) *Inspecting the School Inspectors: New Plans, Old Ills*, London: Centre for Policy Affairs.
Office for Standards in Education (1993) *Handbook for the Inspection of Schools*, London: HMSO.

8 Alternative Education Policies: Assessment and Testing

Paul Black

I have been influenced by research in teacher assessment conducted in the last 25 years (Hewitt 1967, Hoste and Bloomfield 1975, Bloomfield *et al*. 1977, Rudman 1987, Griffin 1989, Hoge and Coladarci 1989, Nitko 1989, Griffin and Nix 1991, Wood 1991), by the several monitoring reports produced about assessment in the shadow of the 1988 Act (those quoted earlier in this article and, in addition, SEAC 1991b, 1992a, Swain 1991a, 1991b, 1992, ASE 1992), and by the critiques, notably the recent outline by the BERA task group on assessment (Harlen *et al*. 1992).

If TGAT fell into one big trap, it was to assume that its radical programme could not only satisfy the political appetites, but that it could survive being implemented at the speed that political pressures demanded. I say this was a trap because the core of TGATs scheme called for radical changes in teachers' practice. Such cannot be achieved within very short time scales by prescription (Fullan 1991). To try to do so is to risk the very dangerous conclusion—'We tried it and we have shown that it cannot work'. Ironically, we may have been fortunate that it was never seriously tried.

References

Allanson, J., Kavanagh, D. and Thomas, N. (1990) 'Assessment and the National Curriculum: The Standing of Teachers and Children'. *The Curriculum Journal* (2), pp.129–37.
ASE Key Stage 3 Monitoring Group 1992 'Report on the Monitoring of Key Stage 3: September 1992'. *Education in Science*, November 1992, pp.18–19.
Bangert-Drowns, R.L., Kulik, J.A. and Kulik, C.C. (1991) 'Effects of Frequent Classroom Testing'. *Journal of Educational Research*, 85 (2), pp.89–99.
Bennett, S.N., Wragg, E.C., Carre, C.G. and Carter, D.G.S. (1992) 'A Longitudinal Study of Primary Teachers' Perceived Competence in, and Concerns About, National Curriculum Implementation'. *Research Papers in Education*, 7(1), pp.53–78.

Black, H. (1986) 'Assessment for Learning'. In Nuttall, D.L. (ed.) *Assessing Educational Achievement*. London: Falmer Press, pp.7–18.

Black, H.D. and Dockrell, W.B. (1982) *Diagnostic Assessment in Secondary Schools*. London: Hodder & Stoughton.

Black, H.D. and Dockrell, W.B. (1984) *Criterion Referenced Assessment in the Classroom*. Edinburgh: Scottish Council for Research in Education.

Black, P.J. (1990) 'APU Science—the Past and the Future'. *School Science Review*. 72(258) pp.13–28.

Black, P.J. (1993) 'The Shifting Scenery of the National Curriculum'. In Simon, B. and Chitty, C. (eds) *Education Answers Back*. London: Lawrence and Wishart, pp.45–60.

Black, P.J. and Simon, S. (1992) *Progression in Learning Science*. Research in Science Education, Melbourne: ASERA, pp.45–54.

Block, J.H., Efthim, H.E. and Burns, R.B. (1989) *Building Effective Mastery Learning in Schools*. White Plains, New York: Longman.

Bloomfield, B., Dobby, J. and Duckworth, D. (1977) 'Mode Comparability in the CSE'. *Schools Council Examination Bulletin 36*. London: Evans/Methuen Educational.

Brown, M. and Denvir, B. (1987) 'The Feasibility of Class Administered Diagnostic Assessment in Primary Mathematics' *Educational Research*. 29(2), pp.95–107.

Butler, J. and Beasley, W. (1987), 'The Impact of Assessment Changes on the Science Curriculum'. *Research in Science Education*. 17, pp.236–43.

Crooks, T.J. (1988) 'The Impact of Classroom Evaluation Practices on Students'. *Review of Educational Research* 58(4), pp.438–81.

DES (1988a) *National Curriculum: Task Group on Assessment and Testing: A Report*. London: Department of Education and Science and Welsh Office.

DES (1988b) *National Curriculum: Task Group on Assessment and Testing: Three Supplementary Reports*. London: Department of Education and Science and Welsh Office.

Ferriman, B. and Lock, R. (1989) 'OCEA: The Development of a Graded-assessment Scheme in Science Part IV: The Pilot Phase'. *School Science Review*, 70(253) pp.97–102.

Fullan, M.G. with Stiegelbauer, S. (1991) *The New Meaning of Educational Change*. London: Cassell.

Griffin, P.E. (1989) *Developing Literacy Profiles*. Coburg 3058, Victoria: Assessment Research Centre, Phillip Institute of Technology.

Griffin, P. and Nix, P. (1991) *Educational Assessment and Reporting: A New Approach*. Marrickville, New South Wales: Harcourt Brace.

Grisay, A. (1991) 'Improving Assessment in Primary Schools: "APER" Research Reduces Failure Rates'. In Weston, P. (ed.) *Assessment of Pupils' Achievement: Motivation and School Success*. Amsterdam: Swets and Zeitlinger, pp.103–18.

Harlen, W. and Qualter, A. (1991) 'Issues in SAT Development and the Practice of Teacher Assessment'. *Cambridge Journal of Education* 21 (2) pp.141–52.

Harlen, W., Gipps, C., Broadfoot, P. and Nuttall, D. (1992) 'Assessment and the Improvement of Education'. *The Curriculum Journal*, 3(3), pp.215–30.

Hewitt, E.A. (1967) *The Reliability of GCE O-level Examinations in English language*. OP 27. Manchester: Joint Matriculation Board.

Hodson, D. (1986) 'The Role of Assessment in the "Curriculum Cycle": a Survey of Science Department Practice'. *Research in Science and Technological Education*. 4(1) pp.7–17.

Hoge, R.D. and Coladarci, T. (1989) 'Teacher-based Judgements of Academic Achievement: A Review of Literature'. *Review of Educational Research*, 59(3) pp.297–313.

Hoste, R. and Bloomfield, B. (1975) 'Continuous Assessment in the CSE: Opinion and Practice'. *Schools Council Examinations Bulletin 31*. London: Evans/Methuen Educational.

Johnson S. (1988), *National Assessment: The APU Science Approach*, London: HMSO.

McCallum, B., McAlister, S., Brown M. and Gipps G. (1994), 'Teacher Assessment at Key Stage One'. *Research Papers in Education*, forthcoming.

Marklund, S. (1991) 'Assessment of Student Achievement in Compulsory and Post-compulsory Schools in Sweden'. In Weston, P. (ed.) *Assessment of Pupils' Achievement: Motivation and School Success*. Amsterdam: Swets and Zeitlinger, pp.31–44.

Murphy, R. and Torrance, H. (1988) *The Changing Face of Educational Assessment*. Milton Keynes: Open University Press.

Nitko, A.J. (1989), 'Designing Tests that are Integrated with Instruction'. In Linn, R.L. (ed.) *Educational Measurement* (3rd edition). London: Collier Macmillan, pp.447–74.

Rudman, H.C. (1987) 'Testing and Teaching: Two Sides of the Same Coin?' *Studies in Educational Evaluation* 13, pp.73–90.

SEAC (1991a) *National Curriculum Assessment: A Report on Teacher Assessment by the NFER/BGC Consortium*. London: Schools Examination and Assessment Council.

SEAC (1991b) *National Curriculum Assessment at Key Stage 1: 1991 Evaluation: Report of the NFER/BGC Consortium*. London: Schools Examination and Assessment Council.

SEAC (1992a) *The Evaluation of National Curriculum Assessment at Key Stage 1: Report of the Leeds ENCA Project*. London: Schools Examination and Assessment Council.

SEAC (1992b) *Teacher Assessment in Mathematics and Science at Key Stage 3: Report by the NFER and Brunel University*. London: Schools Examination and Assessment Council.

Swain, J.R.L. (1989) 'The Development of a Framework for the Assessment of Process Skills in a Graded Assessments in Science Project' *International Journal of Science Education*. 11(3), pp.251–9.

Swain, J.R.L. (1991a) 'Standard Assessment Tasks in Science at Key Stage 3: Initial Development to the 1990 Trial'. *British Journal of Curriculum and Assessment*, 1(2), pp.26–8.

Swain, J.R.L. (1991b) 'Standard Assessment Tasks in Science at Key Stage 3: The 1991 Pilot'. *British Journal of Curriculum and Assessment* 2, pp.19–30.

Swain J.R.L. (1992) 'Trialling and Piloting KS3 Science SATs', *School Science Review*, 74(267) pp.115–20.

Wood, R. (1991) *Assessment and Testing: A Survey of Research*. Cambridge: Cambridge University Press.

9 Towards Education for Democracy

Stewart Ranson

Barry, B. (1989) *Theories of Justice: Volume 1: A Treatise on Social Justice*. London: Harvester Wheatsheaf.

Cordingley, P. and Kogan, M. (1993) *In Support of Education: The Functioning of Local Government*. London: Jessica Kingsley.

DES (1989) *Planning for School Development*. London: HMSO.

Dreze, J. and Sen, A. (1989) *Hunger and Public Action*. Oxford: Clarendon.

Gadamer, H.G. (1975) *Truth and Method*. London: Sheed and Ward.

Gilligan, C. (1986) 'Remapping the Moral Domain'. In Heller, T., Sosna, M. and Wellbury, D. (eds) *Reconstructing Individualism: Autonomy, Individuality and the Self in Western Thought*. Stanford: Stanford University Press.

Glennerster, H. and Low, W. (1990) 'Education and the Welfare State: Does It Add Up?'. In Barr, N. *et al.* (eds), *The State of Welfare: The Welfare State in Britain Since 1974*. Oxford: Clarendon Press.

Habermas, J. (1972) *Knowledge and Human Interests*. London: Heinemann Educational Books.

Habermas, J. (1979) *Communication and the Evolution of Society*. Boston: Beacon Press.

Held, D. (1989) *Political Theory and the Modern State*. Oxford: Polity.

Jordan, B. (1989) *The Common Good: Citizenship, Morality and Self-Interest*. Oxford: Blackwell.

MacIntyre, A. (1981) *After Virtue: A Study in Moral Theory*, London: Duckworth.

Okin, S.M. (1991) 'Gender, the Public and the Private'. In Held, D. (ed.) *Political Theory Today*. Oxford: Polity.

Pateman, C. (1987) 'Feminist Critiques of the Public/Private Dichotomy'. In Phillips, A. (ed.), *Feminism and Equality*. Oxford: Blackwell.

Pring, R. (1987) 'Privatization in Education'. *Journal of Education Policy*, 2(4), pp.289–99.

Ranson, S. (1992a) 'Towards the Learning Society', *Educational Management and Administration*, vol.20.

Ranson, S. (1992b) *The Role of Local Government in Education: Assuring Quality and Accountability*. Harlow: Longman.

Rawls, J. (1971) *A Theory of Justice*. Oxford: Clarendon.

Sen, A. (1990) 'Individual Freedom as Social Commitment'. *New York Review of Books*, 14 June.

Sen, A. (1992) 'On the Darwinian View of Progress', *London Review of Books*, 5 November.

Simey, M. (1985) *Government by Consent: the Principles and Practice of Accountability in Local Government*. London: Bedford Square Press.

Taylor, C. (1985) *Philosophy and the Human Sciences: Philosophical Papers*, 2. Cambridge: Cambridge University Press.

Taylor, C. (1991) *The Ethics of Authenticity*, Cambridge: Harvard University Press.

Taylor, C. (1992) *Multiculturalism and 'The Politics of Recognition'*. Princeton: Princeton University Press.

TES Editorial (1982) 'Church Schools in a Secular Age: What For?', *Times Educational Supplement*. 22 January.

Titmuss, R.M. (1971) *The Gift Relationship: From Human Blood to Social Policy*. London: George Allen and Unwin.

INDEX

178